THE
CHEESE
COMPANION

The Connoisseur's Guide

THE CHEESE COMPANION

The Connoisseur's Guide

BY JUDY RIDGWAY

with a foreword by
ARI WEINZWEIG

RUNNING PRESS
PHILADELPHIA · LONDON

ISBN 0-7624-0500-7

Library of Congress
Cataloging-in-Publication Number
LOC98-67028

This book was designed and produced by
Quintet Publishing Limited
6 Blundell Street
London N7 9BH

CREATIVE DIRECTOR: **richard dewing**
ART DIRECTOR: **clare reynolds**
DESIGN: **balley design associates**
DESIGNERS: **simon balley and joanna hill**
PROJECT EDITOR: **toria leitch**
EDITOR: **rosie hankin**
PHOTOGRAPHER: **ferguson hill**

Typeset in Great Britain by Central Southern Typesetters, Eastbourne
Manufactured in Singapore by Eray Scan Pte Ltd
Printed in China by Leefung-Asco Printers Ltd

This book may be ordered by mail from the publisher.
Please add $2.50 for postage and handling.
But try your bookstore first!

RUNNING PRESS
BOOK PUBLISHERS
125 South Twenty-second Street
Philadelphia Pennsylvania 19103-4399

contents

Foreword by **Ari Weinzweig**

*G*iven a choice of only one food to take into some isolated existence, most folks I know would choose chocolate. Personally, I'd choose cheese. Along with a loaf of good country bread, I could exist on such a diet for days. I can't think of any sort of cheese I wouldn't eat with pleasure, assuming they are well made and properly matured—from fresh creamy, delicate goat cheeses, to classic blue cheeses like Roquefort, Gorgonzola, and Stilton, or new blue cheeses like Maytag or Harbourne. I could eat cheddars from Somerset or Vermont, marvelous well-aged mountain cheeses from the Alps, or creamy Camemberts. If I desired something a little stronger, I would eat the sharp sheep's milk cheeses from southern Italy and central Spain, pungent Pont L'Eveque's, or a two-year-old wedge of what might be the most wonderful cheese in the world, Parmigiano Reggiano. The choices are endless.

I've loved cheese as long as I can remember. However, I grew up in the sixties, in what were likely the darkest of times for great cheese in America. Without question, my favorite childhood cheese was pre-sliced, processed American singles. From there I think I graduated to pre-packed cheddar and sliced swiss (with a small "s" since I'm sure it wasn't from Switzerland!). Fortunately, the last fifteen years have seen an enormous improvement in the range of offerings and today there are dozens of new American cheesemakers in almost every corner of the United States and Canada. Working with goat, sheep, and cow's milk they're crafting a range of new American cheeses; fresh and aged, blue cheeses and cheddars. At the same time, well-deserved attention is again being given to some long-standing American originals, like Dry Jack, Maytag Blue, and Teleme.

With all this in mind, I can confidently say that The Cheese Companion can serve you well as an effective buying guide to cheese. It's small enough to slip into your coat pocket; light enough to carry to the market; easy enough to use discreetly while you're standing, front and center, at your local cheese shop. This book offers interested cheese eaters and cheese buyers easy access to important background and buying information. In the hands of a curious and concerned consumer, The Cheese Companion can help raise the standards of the quality of cheese shops all over America. Read, taste, experiment, and indulge. The fine flavors of the world of cheese are waiting. I hope you enjoy your cheese education as much as I've enjoyed mine.

part one

The story of cheese

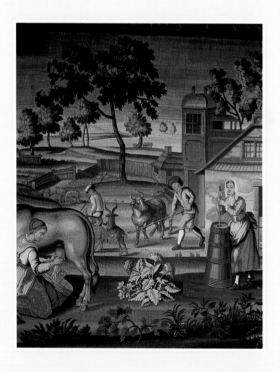

History

No one knows exactly when or where cheese was first made. Like so many inventions, cheesemaking was probably discovered by different communities at about the same time. We do know that sheep were domesticated around twelve thousand years ago and that cows were raised in Ancient Egypt. It seems reasonable to suppose that cheese came into being soon after these animals were domesticated for their milk.

Milk was kept in containers of leather, porous pottery, or wood. Since such containers would have been difficult to keep clean, the new milk must have soured very quickly. The next step would have been to drain the whey from the curds to make a simple kind of fresh cheese. This may well have been how the first cheese came to be made. As these early cheeses did not use rennet, they must have been fairly sharp and acidic.

Using rennet to curdle milk without souring was a big step forward in cheesemaking. The origins of this process, too, are obscure but by the third or fourth century BC cheesemaking was much more sophisticated. In Europe, by Roman times, molding and pressing techniques had been added to the use of rennet, and the hard cheesemaking process was much the same as that in use today.

Roman soldiers received a regular ration of cheese along with other staples such as bread, wine, and salt. So wherever a fort was established, cheesemaking would follow. Thus the art of cheesemaking spread throughout the empire.

As the Middle Ages wore on, religious foundations across Europe became great centers of agricultural activity because they were major landowners. Cheese was very important for the many fast days when it was forbidden to eat meat. The various orders and religious houses developed many different kinds of cheese, perhaps to add interest to their often limited diet. Many of today's well-known cheeses were originally associated with a monastery or convent. Wensleydale, Pont l'Évêque, and Tête de Moine are good examples of such cheeses. From the late medieval period to the late nineteenth century, cheesemaking in the various European countries continued to develop along distinctive lines. Hard cheeses came to predominate in the mountains of Switzerland and the hills and valleys of Britain, while softer cheeses with washed and mold rinds became the hallmark of France.

With the growth of trade and the increasingly urban population, cheese became a highly regarded and economically important commodity. Cheeses began to be traded not only outside their own areas of production but also across borders, and when Europeans colonized the New World they took their cheesemaking traditions with them.

All cheese was, of course, made with raw milk but in the 1850s the French microbiologist, Louis Pasteur, invented the pasteurization process, and cheesemaking changed for all time. Raw milk contains microorganisms which, if the cheesemaker is not extremely careful, can not only spoil the cheese but infect the eater. As a result cheesemaking was a small-scale and labour-intensive art.

Pasteurization allowed large-scale cheese production for the very first time. Milk from different locations and different herds could be mixed together to achieve a standardized product and the risk of fault-producing organisms was cut right back. The producers could use their own carefully developed starter cultures and exert far more control over the production process.

The last hundred years have seen the formalizing of these scientifically based techniques with large factory-style creameries taking over from the small, more traditional dairies. Cheesemakers in many countries have copied the world's most successful cheeses and are mass-producing them on a very large scale. The result has been a down-grading of the individuality and quality of cheese generally.

France

Even in Roman times France had the reputation for producing some of the best cheeses in the world. Roquefort and Cantal cheeses were taken to Rome for the delectation of the wealthy citizens and are probably the cheeses referred to by Pliny the Elder in his *Historia Naturalis* written in the first century AD.

Earlier cheeses may have been made in shallow pottery bowls known as "mortaria." The rough inner surface of these bowls could have retained the curd-forming bacteria from one day to the next, removing the need for rennet, herbs, or old whey to set the milk working. The whey was poured off through the small spout. Cream cheese is still made in this way in some parts of France.

above: *The ripening of Cantal.*

How closely the Roquefort and Cantal of Roman times resembled their modern counterparts is not known but it is likely that the cheesemaking traditions of these areas were kept alive after the Romans left. Certainly during the seventh and eighth centuries, cheesemaking was continued in the monasteries. This was much encouraged by Charlemagne, King of the Franks and later Holy Roman Emperor, and there are numerous stories of this enlightened monarch trying new cheeses and demanding to be sent a yearly supply.

By medieval times cheese-production was well established for Brie and Comté, as well as for Roquefort and Cantal, and the monasteries were developing new cheeses such as Munster, Maroilles, and Livarot. This activity was encouraged by the courtly custom of sending a gift of cheese to those one admired or wanted to impress. Blanche of Navarre is reputed to have sent two hundred cheeses to the King of France every year, and the poet Charles d'Orléans sent cheese to ladies whom he admired.

Local cheesemaking by peasant farmers was also on the increase and as new methods and techniques were introduced so the choice grew. Sheep's and goat's milk were the basis of much local cheese-making but as time went on cow's milk, which was available all year round, became increasingly important. Local cheesemakers jealously guarded their secret methods and many of them successfully protected their cheeses by legal means. Local authenticity for some thirty-two cheeses is still guaranteed today by means of the Appellation d'Origine system which can be seen on the label (left) (see page 38).

Until the fifteenth century, the part played by cheese in the diet of the average French family was determined by that family's place in the social hierarchy. The poor ate fresh or briefly matured cheese as an everyday item. The rich ate cheese as a novelty to titillate the palate at the end of a large meal. The latter could afford to wait for a cheese to mature for six, eight, or even twelve months. By the late sixteenth century, however, fresh cheese had become much more fashionable among the rich and very rich. Not only were they served at the cheese course, but also used in elaborate desserts and many fancy pastries.

The French have always enjoyed the good things in life, and this includes food and drink. So it is not surprising that their many local cheeses have survived for so long. There is currently said to be more than one French cheese for each day of the year.

French producers took advantage of the advent of pasteuriz-ation but *fermier* or farm-produced cheese has, until recently, always been the benchmark for the *laitier* or factory-produced cheese. Lately there has been some blurring of standards as the creameries have created their own cheeses with nothing to act as a point of comparison. Many of these cheeses are rather bland, though some have gained a good following in France too.

right: *The ubiquitous combination; cheese and wine.*

[11]

United Kingdom

Britain was certainly producing hard cheeses during the Roman occupation, and Cheshire cheese is recorded as being on sale in Rome itself. Indeed the Romans liked it so much that they were prepared to go to great lengths to get the recipe. There is a story that the Romans hanged a cheesemaker at Chester for refusing to give it to them.

above: *Bonchester cows in Roxburghshire.*

It is likely that simple soft cheeses had been made in shallow bowls, similar to those in use in France, before the Romans landed. During the Dark Ages, cheesemaking in Britain again reverted to these primitive methods. However, the more sophisticated techniques of hard cheese production were not entirely lost and the Celts of Wales and Ireland probably continued to make hard cheese. With the spread of Christianity and the growth of the monasteries, cheesemaking flourished once again.

Cheesemaking at this time was a summer activity because cows were largely slaughtered before the winter. Until the sixteenth century, sheep's and goat's milk were as widespread as cow's milk and even Cheddar was probably originally made with both sheep's and cow's milk.

Medieval cheeses were classified by texture, not by place of origin. There was very little trading activity during these times and cheeses were sold almost exclusively in their own areas. The various techniques became firmly established and remained so to the twentieth century.

Hard cheese was made from skim milk and it was very hard indeed. Long keeping made it even worse. It was known as "white meat," and destined for servants and farm laborers. Semihard cheese, made from whole or low-fat milk and matured for a shorter time, was much more palatable. Fresh cheese was a luxury product available only to the lord of the manor.

SUFFOLK CHEESE

The worst of the medieval hard cheeses came from the butter-producing regions of Essex and Suffolk. A rude little rhyme about Suffolk cheeses ran:

"Those that made me were uncivil,
They made me harder than the devil.
Knives won't cut me, fire won't sweat me,
Dogs bark at me, but can't eat me."

Hard cheese began to lose its bad reputation during the seventeenth century when cow's milk virtually superseded all other kinds and the traditional cheeses of Britain gradually established themselves. Merchants, factors, and peddlers bought up the best cheeses at country markets in Somerset, Gloucestershire, and Lancashire, and sold them in other parts of the country where the cheese was not so good.

Toward the end of the seventeenth century, the London cheesemongers formed an unofficial guild and began to ship cheeses by river and canal, and even by sea over relatively long distances. Cheddar began to build up its reputation. At

right: *A Medieval tapestry showing a woman milking cattle.*

first it appeared only on the tables of the rich but when the farmers banded together into cooperatives, they were able to make more cheese and sell it at a lower price.

Stilton was first referred to in 1725 by Daniel Defoe. He was touring England and Wales, passed through Stilton, and sampled the cheese. Surprisingly there are no obvious references specifically to blue cheese before Daniel Defoe, though there must always have been some cheese which naturally turned blue such as the Blue Wensleydale made by the monks of Jervaulx Abbey in Yorkshire.

STILTON MAKERS ASSOC. CHEESE

Certification Trade Mark

above: *The logo of the Stilton Cheesemakers' Association.*

Stilton, so-called "king of cheeses," has never been made in the village of Stilton, though it came to fame at the Bell Inn in the village. The inn was supplied with the cheese by a certain Elizabeth Scarbrow and subsequently by her daughter and granddaughter. The original recipe came from nearby Quemby Hall where Elizabeth was housekeeper and where it was known as Lady Beaumont's cheese. It is now the only English cheese to be protected by a copyright invested in the Stilton Cheesemakers' Association.

Stilton used to be ripened far beyond what would be acceptable today. Defoe records that it was brought to the table with mites or maggots so thickly clustered over it that a spoon was brought to eat it. Nevertheless, it gained in popularity and the Bell Inn was able to sell Stilton at two shillings and sixpence a pound, a price which was not to be equalled again until the middle of the twentieth century.

Scotland made a little fresh cheese like Caboc, the recipe for which dates back to the fifteenth century, but largely preferred to turn its milk into butter. This probably accounts for the fact that Dunlop, Scotland's only traditional hard cheese, is very much a variation on the Cheddar theme.

Cheesemaking in Ireland continued with a small production of a mixture of fresh and mature cheeses which has today blossomed into a range of very good farmhouse cheeses.

The nineteenth century saw a great expansion in British cheesemaking as scientists began to understand the process of fermentation. Pasteurization and factory techniques sadly swept away far more of the old farmhouse traditions than they had in France or Spain. For many years the great British cheeses were at best mediocre and at worst simply bad.

However, the late twentieth century saw a revival of small-scale cheesemaking and an increasing demand for well-made full-flavored cheese. It is now possible to buy traditional cheeses which are handmade in the farm dairy. There is also a plethora of new farmhouse cheeses made from a range of cow's, sheep's, and goat's milk. So it is now possible to find local cheeses almost everywhere.

above: *Cropwell Bishop Village, with the Creamery building on the left-hand side of the road.*

Italy

Cheesemaking had a good start in Italy. The early Romans had an aversion to fresh milk, preferring to turn it into cheese. The milk came mainly from goats and ewes, and fig juice was used to curdle it. With the introduction of rennet, cheese-making became more sophisticated and by the first century BC there was a wide variety of cheese from which to choose. Roman soldiers were given a portion of cheese a day as part of their rations. The Romans used cheese a great deal in cooking, and characteristic dishes included cheese and honey baked in pastry, bread, cakes made with cheese, and even cheese-flavored sweetmeats.

Fresh cheese, often flavored with herbs or spices, and smoked cheeses, were extremely popular and were served by day or night as snacks or as part of a more formal meal. Rennet-curdled, spun, and dried cheeses, and the grainy textured *grana* cheeses, like Parmesan, were developed early on. The rich were also able to add French, Greek, and even British cheeses to their cheese boards. During the Dark Ages, religious communities, particularly in the Po Valley, kept the cheese-making traditions going. By the thirteenth century, Gorgonzola and Parmesan were well established. As the monks extended the water meadows of the Po to provide lush grazing, cow's milk gradually took over from ewe's milk as the base material for these cheeses.

One of the earliest references to Parmesan is found in the fourteenth-century stories

below: *Mozzarella being salted in a brine solution.*

of Boccaccio's *Decameron*. One character tells another about the "whole mountain of Parmesan cheese, all finely grated, on top of which stood people who were doing nothing but making macaroni and ravioli." He adds that all these delicacies were being "rolled into the cheese after cooking, the better to season them."

The rest of Italy does not have such sweet meadowland as the Po Valley and in many areas sheep remained the main source of milk for cheese. As a result Tuscany, Lazio, Campania, Sardinia, Puglia, and Sicily are all renowned for their ewe's milk cheeses, which are known under the general name of Pecorino.

above: *Mixing and cutting the curds.*

In fact, the geography of Italy is so diverse that the range of cheeses produced begins to rival that of France. In the north, alpine meadows produce their own particular type of mountain cheese, whereas the swamps of the south offer an ideal climate for water buffalo, whose milk has traditionally been used for Mozzarella.

No one quite knows where the water buffalo first came from. One theory is that they arrived in Italy with the Longobards around AD596 . Alternatively they could simply be indigenous to the region. In fact, until the beginning of the nineteenth century, buffalo rearing was widespread in many Italian regions. The animals were left in the countryside in a semiwild state, being gathered in at dawn for milking.

As in France the local strength of Italian cheesemaking traditions, and the high regard in which the Italians hold good cheese, have ensured that quality cheese production continues despite the advance of factory-based production methods.

Switzerland

Swiss cheese has a history as long and distinguished as that of French cheese. Many centuries before the birth of Christ, the Celtic ancestors of the Swiss used to make cheese in rough vessels slung over wood fires, cutting and stirring the curds with branches of pine. The resultant cheese had a tough rind which was impenetrable enough to thwart the ravages of both time and the weather.

This Celtic cheese was ideal for the lonely mountain life, where the snows could isolate small communities for months on end, and it was probably the forerunner of the much-imitated mountain cheeses like Gruyère and Emmental.

The first mention of Gruyère appears in the year 1115 in the books of the Abbey of Rougemont near Gruyère. Another very old cheese is Vacherin Fribourgeois, not to be confused with Vacherin Mont d'Or. It was served to visiting royalty as long ago as 1448.

Cheese was regarded as a gauge of social standing in Switzerland. The age and quantity of the cheese in the family cellar was seen as an indication of prosperity. This was not so surprising in a community that used cheese as currency, paying priests, artisans, and workers partly in cash and partly in fine cheese. Cheese was even used as a traditional gift at the birth of a child.

The Swiss have traded their cheeses since Roman times and some of them have become so popular abroad that steps had to be taken to protect the home market.

Unpasteurized milk is used in Swiss cheesemaking and the tradition of fine farmhouse cheeses has weathered the introduction of factory production more successfully than in many countries. The Swiss cheeses included in this book are controlled by regional cooperatives which are in turn regulated by a national council. No region is allowed to make cheese that is not designated as original to that region.

right: *A selection of Swiss cheeses.*

The Netherlands and Germany

The first known records of cheesemaking in The Netherlands are from the ninth century AD. These show that cheese destined for the court of Charlemagne was made in Friesland.

During the Middle Ages, cheesemaking became really well established, with special cheese weigh-houses or *Kaaswaag* for regulating the size and weight of the cheeses being established in Haarlem, Linden, and Leeuwarden.

The early Dutch cheese-makers developed cheeses which had exceptional keeping qualities. They were extremely reliable and easy to transport. As a result they were sent overland to Germany and then by sea to the far corners of the Baltic and the Mediterranean. Exports continued through the centuries to places as far afield as the Dutch East Indies and South America. Today Dutch cheese exports have become so successful that Holland is—to many people—synonymous with cheese.

above: *The famous cheese market at Alkmaar, Holland, where Gouda and Edam are displayed for sale.*

Hard cheese is made in Germany but homemade fresh cheese made without rennet was the tradition for centuries. Indeed Quark, the modern version of this type of cheese, still accounts for around half of German cheese production. Rennet was introduced in the Middle Ages but the German hard cheeses on sale today date back no further than a hundred and fifty years or so. Very few of these cheeses are indigenous; most are copies of cheese from other lands. Limburg cheese, for example, came originally from Belgium; Münster comes from France; and Allgau Emmenthaler is based on the Swiss original.

All cheese in The Netherlands and in Germany is made, by law, from pasteurized milk. Production is mostly in very large factories.

Scandinavia

Cow's milk and cheese are probably not the first items that spring to mind on hearing mention of the Vikings. However, Vikings captured by the Moors of Spain in the ninth century AD are said to have saved their lives by telling their captors all they knew about cheesemaking. The Vikings certainly knew about cattle, and they introduced new breeds into Europe, some of which provided the bloodlines of modern breeds

above: *Cumin seeds, traditionally used to flavor cheese.*

such as Guernsey and Gloucester cows and the large brown cattle of Normandy. The Vikings traveled with their bulls and cows on their longships, and these interbred with native cattle where they settled.

The earliest cheeses to make any impact on Scandinavia were probably made in Denmark where primitive tribes kept goats, sheep, and cattle. But, despite this early start, Denmark has not established many individual cheeses. Like Germany, most of its cheeses are derivative. Nevertheless, cheesemaking was an occupation to be proud of; the larger the cheese, the greater the professional skill of the maker. Some cheeses were so large that several men could hardly lift them.

In Norway and Sweden the early cheeses were strongly flavored, long-lasting cheeses, such as Gammalost, which sustained the Norsemen on their long sea voyages. Smoked cheese and cheeses spiced with cumin seeds or cloves were also popular for their keeping qualities.

Up until the eighteenth century, food was commonly used as currency to pay taxes levied by the Church. In areas where pasture was owned by the Church, milk or cheese was the required payment. The parson then made more cheese with the milk and traded the cheeses for other commodities. Such cheeses became known as *Prastost* or "parsonage" cheeses.

Today Scandinavian cheese production is factory based using pasteurized milk.

Spain and Portugal

Spain has sharply contrasting areas of climate. In central and southern Spain, it is hot and arid; in the northwest along the Cantabrian mountains and into Galicia, there are verdant valleys and hills with good grazing land. But both regions have, in the past, been essentially sheep country and Spain's traditional cheeses were all made with ewe's or goat's milk.

However, in recent years milk from cows raised in the northwest and on the Balearic Islands has begun to gain ground. Some is used to make new cheeses but some also goes into the production of established cheeses, like Cabrales and Picon, which are now often made from a mixture of different milks.

At one time Spain consumed all her own cheese at home but this is gradually changing and Spanish cheeses are finding their way onto the international market. Perhaps because of this late flowering, Spain only brought in a denomination of origin system for cheese in 1981.

Portuguese cheeses are even less well known outside Portugal than Spanish cheeses. This is because the quantities of cheese produced are small, yet the Portuguese demand for cheese is large. Most cheese is home produced. Even Queijo de Serra or "mountain cheese," the country's most important cheese, is made on small farms from raw goat's or ewe's milk. The cheese is interesting because most farmers do not use rennet but prefer to make their own cultures from the flowers and leaves of a thistle species that grows wild. At their best these cheeses can be very good indeed.

below: *The countryside around Galicia.*

The United States

The United States is now the largest producer of cheese in the world, yet the cheese industry only started in 1851. In that year Jesse Williams opened the first Cheddar cheese factory in Oneida County, New York State. Many more factories have opened since then, producing different cheeses but Cheddar or Cheddar-based cheeses account for the lion's share of all cheese produced.

There are very few "American" cheeses and it could be argued that even Colby and Jack take their inspiration from Cheddar, and that Brick and Leiderkranz are reminiscent of Limburg. This is not really very surprising since every cheese came from another country. The first cheeses to be made were those with which the immigrants were familiar from their previous homes. Perhaps because of the lack of traditional cheese, Americans consume the undemanding cheeses on sale in most supermarkets, and so they use large quantities of processed (Cheddar) cheese and imitation and substitute cheeses.

However pioneering cheese-sellers are gradually wooing the public back to an appreciation of good cheese, not only by importing from Europe but also by encouraging the first-class producers that do exist in the United States itself. Tillamook Cheddar from Oregon, Vella's Bear Flag Dry Jack from California, Maytag Blue from Iowa, and Old Kentucky Tomme bear witness to that. In addition there is a growing number of small producers making a range of exciting fresh and aged goat's milk cheeses.

above: *The Maytag Dairy Farm in Iowa.*

Australia and New Zealand

Cheesemaking began in New South Wales during the early part of the nineteenth century and it was Cheddar that was made. Other states soon followed and, for a hundred years or more, Cheddar was made to various states of maturity on the farms.

As immigrants from countries other than Britain arrived in Australia, so different cheesemaking techniques were introduced, and now there are copies of cheeses from many other parts of Europe.

New Zealand also has a flourishing cheesemaking industry and New Zealanders have turned to making all kinds of different cheeses. Nevertheless Cheddar remains paramount in both countries.

The Rest of the World

Canada is not a big cheese-eating or cheese-producing country though its excellent Cheddar does find its way round the world.

Belgium and Austria have always produced good cheese, but they have tended to be rather overshadowed by their neighbors. Belgium is now busy, however, producing a new range of modern factory cheeses.

Cheese is quite important in Greece and the Balkans where herds of sheep and goats provide the milk. Today a good deal of the cheese on sale is made up of simple brined, fresh cheese like Feta. There are also pressed and matured cheeses like Kefalotiri and Haloumi. The latter originated in the Arab world and is still made in Turkey, Cyprus, and the rest of the Middle East. Russia produces considerable quantities of cheese but none of it is exported.

In South Africa immigrants from Britain and The Netherlands each brought their own cheesemaking traditions and so Cheddar and Dutch-style cheeses like Gouda are predominant. There are also a few farmhouse cheeses being made on wine estates and farms.

The knowledge of cheesemaking found its way east as well as west from Asia Minor but remained very basic. India, for example, makes a simple curd cheese known as Paneer.

The South Americans never really acquired the cheese habit, preferring to rear their cattle for meat. In Central America, Africa, and parts of Southeast Asia the climate is too hot for successful cheesemakings, which meant that here too cheese never became part of the daily diet.

How Cheese is Made

*T*he principles of cheesemaking are the same for all but the simplest of unripened fresh cheese, but within these principles there is room for endless variety. This is where the cheesemakers' art comes in. Their skill has produced the hundreds of different cheeses from which we are now able to choose.

In essence, cheese is made by removing the water or whey from milk and allowing the resulting milk solids or curds to spoil in a controlled manner. Collecting and preparing the milk is the first stage in this process. The second stage is the production of curds, and the third the concentration of these curds by cutting, cooking, and salting. Finally the cheese is ripened.

Each of these stages is crucial not only to producing good quality cheese, but also in determining what kind of cheese is produced. For example, the way in which the curds are cut will affect the texture of the cheese, and the method of salting will affect the way in which the cheese ripens.

Cheesemaking is such a complex process, and the treatment of each cheese so critical, that even two cheeses which start off from the same batch of milk and undergo the same processes will not necessarily taste exactly the same. Of course, this is one of the attractions of real farmhouse cheese. Only the mass manufacturer aims to make all cheeses of the same type taste the same.

Collecting and Preparing the Milk

Small-scale producers collect raw milk from their own animals or from nearby farms; factories receive it by the tanker load. Either way it must be kept as clean as possible and this can be quite difficult, particularly if the milk comes from a number of different sources. Most small producers use the raw untreated milk but large-scale producers nearly always pasteurize their milk.

Milk is a raw material that differs from one batch to another, and these differences will manifest themselves in the finished product—the cheese. So pasteurization is also used by the larger manufacturers to standardize the milk to fit their specific process.

The result is a uniform product, consistently clean and pleasant, but devoid of any real character.

Small cheesemakers, on the other hand, revel in these differences. They may get the odd failure but they will also reach the heights of texture and taste. Most cheese connoisseurs believe that the contrast between cheese made from unpasteurized milk and pasteurized milk is like the difference between fine wine and regular table wine. They argue that pasteurization inactivates the natural enzymes in the milk which would normally help the final flavor of the cheese to develop. The process also retards the action of the rennet which means that the curd needs longer ripening in order to achieve the full flavor and texture of the cheese.

Some countries, like Denmark, Germany, and The Netherlands, have passed laws which state that cow's milk cheese be made only from pasteurized milk. The United States makes the same demand for cheeses which are matured for fewer than sixty days. Other countries are resisting such laws on the grounds that cheese made from unpasteurized milk is not a health hazard if due care is taken to adhere to stringent standards of hygiene in the dairy. Indeed, there have been fewer health problems associated with cheese made from unpasteurized milk that with that made from pasteurized milk. Even the few recorded cases of listeria caused by

above: *A cow being milked at the farm in Bonchester Bridge.*

above: *Cutting the curds.*

cheese have nearly all been traced back to pasteurized, not unpasteurized, cheese. Most of the world's cheese is now made from cow's milk which is easily available all year round. But there are also many cheeses which are made from ewe's and goat's milk. Water buffalo, yaks, and camels are also milked for cheese, but today only in relatively remote areas.

We tend to think of milk as just "milk" but it can and does vary quite considerably. Different breeds of cattle produce very differently flavored milk. The food the animal has been eating, the soil on which its pasture is growing, and even the weather on the day the animal is milked all affect the milk itself. Milk produced toward the end of the milking is higher in fats than that at the beginning and there is also a difference between morning and evening milk. Summer milk is reputed to produce better cheese because it tends to be richer than winter milk. The small cheese-maker will take all these factors into account when making cheese.

Sheep and goats can live in countryside which is not suitable for cattle and the use of their milk allows cheese to be made where it would not otherwise be possible. Goat's milk is largely free of the microorganisms which cause disease and it is rarely pasteurized. In the past milk from these animals was only available during the first half of the year. So the availability of fresh cheese was restricted to these months with longer-ripening cheeses on sale for a few months more. Some producers now use frozen goat milk or frozen curds to extend their cheese production period. Others, with larger herds, have developed out-of-season breeding systems.

The first step in cheesemaking is to pool the milk in one or more large containers. At this stage cream may be added to make a richer mix or the milk may be partly or even fully skimmed to make a lower-fat cheese.

If the milk is to be pasteurized it will typically be heated to 160°F and kept at that temperature for 15 seconds. The process affects the flavor of the milk which in turn gives a slightly cooked taste to cheeses made from it. To avoid this problem, some creameries use a more gentle heat treatment, heating the milk to 114°F and holding it there for 30 minutes.

Some cheeses have natural dyes, such as annatto, added to the milk to color them. Others are flavored with herbs or spices, such as sage or cumin seeds, though these may be added later. The different producing countries vary in their laws on what can be added to cheese.

Producing the Curds

If left to itself, raw milk will sour naturally but the process is very unpredictable. Pasteurized milk will not sour in this way. So, whatever the milk, a starter culture of special bacteria is added to change the milk sugars (lactose) into lactic acid. This increases the acidity level of the milk so that the milk protein (casein) will form curds when a coagulating agent, usually rennet, is added.

After the starter culture has been added, the cheesemaker constantly tests the acidity level of the milk so that he or she knows just when to add the rennet. Once this has been added the protein molecules lump together to form a soft jelly or junket-like gel. They are then allowed to settle at a fixed temperature for anything from 30 minutes to two hours.

The temperatures used vary from 70°F through 95°F and depend upon the kind of cheese being made. Low temperatures result in soft curds for a soft cheese and high temperatures in the harder, rubbery curds needed for semihard cheeses. Medium temperatures are used for hard cheeses like Cheddar. Some cheeses like Quark and Fromage Frais are coagulated entirely by lactic acid formation and no rennet is used.

RENNET

Animal rennet is obtained from the lining of the appropriate animal's stomach but modern research has now enabled highly concentrated vegetable rennet to be used instead. In the past, vegetable rennet from a variety of plants was used but it was not sufficiently strong to curdle the quantities of milk used in mass production.

Concentrating the Curds

Separating the curds from the whey and concentrating them is the next stage and the different ways of doing this vary according to the type of cheese being made.

First, the curds are cut to release the whey. How this is done determines the moisture content and so the texture of the finished cheese. Thus for softer cheese, the curds are cut sparingly and ladled into mounds to be drained naturally. The curds for some cheese such as Camembert are hardly cut at all. For harder cheeses, the curds may be cut vertically and horizontally into tiny pieces or combed into thin strands. This releases a good deal more liquid and results in a firmer, drier cheese. As the small pieces of curd fall to the bottom of the vat, they cling together again to form a solid mass and this may be cut again to give a crumbly texture to the cheese.

Cheddaring is the name given to a specific method of cutting

below left: *Ladling the curds from the vat to the tray.*
below right: *The cheddaring process.*

the curds to achieve a fine and smooth Cheddar-cheeselike texture. The curds are cut into large blocks like cinder blocks and piled one on top of the other up the side of the vat. The idea is to expel as much whey as possible without cutting the curd too much.

As well as cutting the curds, the cheesemaker may also heat or cook them. Heat changes the texture of the curd making it much denser and a lot more compact. The resulting cheese

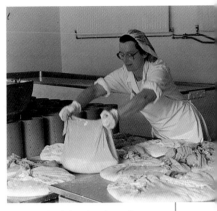

above: *Draining the cheese in cheesecloth.*

will have a firmer texture and be aged for longer than uncooked cheese. Temperatures vary from 105°F, for cheeses like Fontina, to 120°F or more for Gruyère and Emmental. Mozzarella and Provolone are cut and heated until the curd can be pulled into tender strings. The curd is then kneaded and stretched in order to compact the structure even more. These cheeses are known as spun or "pasta filata" cheeses.

Once the whey has been drained off it, too, can be used to make cheese. Swedish Mesost is one example and Italian Ricotta used to be another, but now this more likely to be made from skim or even full-cream milk.

A good many cheeses are now put into perforated molds to continue draining and to ripen. These molds can be of any shape or size, and many are traditional. They are made of a variety of materials, such as wood, stainless steel, basketware, or cheesecloth. The cheeses may be left to firm naturally or they may be lightly or heavily pressed. Of course, the harder the cheese is pressed, the firmer the paste will be.

All cheeses, except the softest cream and cottage cheeses, are salted. The salt changes the acidity level of the cheese and slows down the activity of the starter bacteria, thus controlling the rate at which the cheese later ripens. It also helps to suppress the growth of spoilage bacteria. The salt may be added to the milled

left: *The temperature and humidity makes caves ideal for storing cheese.*

curd, as in Cheddar cheese, or granules may be rubbed onto the surface of the formed cheese, as in the manufacture of Parmesan and Roquefort. Alternatively the whole cheese may be soaked in brine after molding. This method is used for Emmental cheese and some of the other Swiss cheeses. Finally some cheeses, such as Taleggio and Livarot, are rubbed or "washed" on the outside with a brine-soaked cloth. A few cheeses, like Greek Feta cheese, are so heavily salted that all bacterial activity is stopped and it will not benefit from any further ripening.

Ripening the Cheese

Ripening is a very involved process in which the microbes and enzymes in the cheese slowly change its chemical composition from complex organic molecules into much simpler ones. The cheese starts to take on its own special texture and flavor.

This very important curing process takes place in caves or, failing that, in special storage rooms where the temperature and the humidity are carefully controlled. The temperature is kept fairly low to make sure that the desirable organisms included in the starter culture grow at a slow and steady rate. Too fast a growth results in uneven maturing and the production of unwanted chemicals. The humidity, on the other hand, is kept quite high, at around 80 percent for hard cheeses and 95 percent for soft cheeses. This prevents the surface of the cheese drying out.

Soft cheeses, like Camembert, Coulommiers, and Brie, ripen quickly so they are ripened at lower temperatures than hard cheeses. Soft cheeses ripen from the outside in. Some have a

Penicillium mold added to the starter culture, others are sprayed with the mold. In both cases the molds produce a soft bloomy crust on the outside of the immature cheese which then continues to work on the paste inside.

Mold rind cheeses look quite different when they are unwrapped at home than the way they looked in the storage room. The packaging flattens the soft furry down of the mold growth. As the cheese ages, the paste starts to soften nearest to the rind, the center being the last part to lose its chalkiness. The French call this chalky center *l'âme* or the soul of the cheese.

Other soft, and some semihard, cheeses are washed in brine, wine, beer, or spirits and the liquid acts as food for the surface bacteria. These cheeses usually have a characteristic reddish color to their rind and a very pronounced aroma. The flavor may also be fairly pungent, but more often is very much less smelly than the actual rind.

Blue cheeses like Stilton and Roquefort also ripen from within. The mold culture can be introduced with the starter cultures or be added at the curd stage. The ripening cheeses are pierced with metal skewers to introduce oxygen into the interior of the cheese. This feeds the molds which eventually produce blue veins in the paste.

above: *A soft white rind is produced on cheeses such as Brie during the ripening process.*

The very first blue cheeses were probably the result of accidental contamination by microbes naturally occurring in a particular area. The Roquefort caves, for example, harbor one predominant mold. Until comparatively recently, blue cheese could be made only where these molds were present. Today cultures can be prepared and sent anywhere in the world.

Even with modern techniques, making a blue cheese is even more difficult than making other cheeses. The growth of molds within the cheese can be unpredictable. However, the cheesemaker can delay the development of the mold by sealing the cheese and withholding air. Then when he or she feels it is time for the mold to start growing, the cheese will be pierced to allow the air back in and help the veins to develop and spread.

Hard cheeses, too, ripen from the inside out. They take much longer to mature than soft cheeses and are usually kept at slightly higher temperatures. Some of them are brushed and scraped or rubbed with oil. Others are wrapped in bandages to encourage mold growth. This was the traditional way to ripen Cheddar cheese. Today Cheddar cheese made by the mass producers and by some large farmhouse dairies is wrapped in plastic to mature. Plastic prevents air getting to the cheese and so cheese which is ripened in this way will taste different. However, if the cheesemaker knows his or her job, the cheese can still have an excellent flavor.

The length of time it is left to ripen is very important to the texture and flavor of a cheese. Cheddar cheeses which have been matured for six to eight months taste quite different than those matured for twelve to eighteen months. Texture too can change considerably during the ripening

left: *Rubbing the cheese smooth to stop the early ingress of air and premature growth of mold.*

above: *Traditional blue cheeses are characterized by a firm texture and a strong flavor.*

process. For example, if Propionibacter bacteria are included in the starter culture, as they are for Emmental, the cheese will develop quite large holes in the paste. The reason for this is that these bacteria live on lactic acid and as they consume it they give off carbon dioxide. This eventually disappears, leaving the holes behind.

Hard cheeses are turned at regular intervals during ripening to ensure even development. Cheesemakers also check the color, odor, shape, texture, and even the sound of their cheeses, and a cheese iron is used to check on plugs taken from the inside of the cheese.

Most cheese is matured where it is made but some cheese is bought by specialty cheese shops before it is ready to sell. They then store it in their own cold cellars and look after it themselves until it reaches the level of maturity they and their customers require.

Once a cheese is pronounced ready for the table, it is either sold at once or coated to prevent moisture loss, spoilage, and physical damage. Cloth, wax, foil, paper, and plastic are all used for this purpose with varying degrees of success. Paper may not be enough to stop the cheese drying out. On the other hand plastic does not allow the cheese to breathe and it may sweat.

Classifying Cheese

*M*any attempts have been made to classify cheese. Some systems concentrate on production processes, others on texture or type of rind. Some systems have even been based on how smelly it is. In fact, it is very difficult to classify cheese without having to keep listing exceptions. Because the recipes are so many and varied, it is also perfectly possible for one cheese to belong to more than one class.

Here are three methods of classifying cheese which may be of some help when reading labels, shelf descriptions, and choosing cheese from a catalog.

Texture of the Cheese

This can be quite a useful indication of the style of cheese to expect. It is directly related to the water content of the cheese: the softer the cheese the higher its water content. Of course, there is some overlap. It also becomes more complicated because cheese loses water as it matures. Some cheeses may be soft when they are made, but much harder when they are mature. Small goat cheeses are a good example.

VERY SOFT *(80 percent water)* Spoonable cheeses, including almost all fresh cheeses, except Feta.

SOFT *(50–70 percent water)* Spreadable cheeses, including Brie, Camembert, Pont l'Évêque, Reblochon, and Taleggio.

SEMIHARD *(40–50 percent water)* Sliceable cheeses with a slightly rubbery texture, including Tilsit, Gouda, and Port Salut.

SEMIHARD BLUE *(40–50 percent*

left: *Hard cheeses are produced by the loss of moisture during the ripening process.*

above: *Washed rind cheeses.*

water) Crumbly or springy cheese, the former perhaps being difficult to slice, including Roquefort, Stilton, and Bleu d'Auvergne.

HARD *(30–50 percent water)* Firm and very slightly crumbly, firm and slightly rubbery, or very firm and dense cheeses, including Cheddar and Lancashire (firm and crumbly), Gruyère and Emmental (firm and slightly rubbery), and Parmesan and aged Pecorino (very firm and dense).

Cheese rinds

The rind of a cheese controls the progression of water from inside the cheese to the outside and of air into the cheese. It also regulates the release of gases from the cheese.

WHITE MOLD RINDS In fast ripening cheeses the white mold is left to grow unhindered. The rind will not be very thick and can usually be eaten. In other cases the growing mold is brushed off from time to time to produce a thicker rind. This too is edible. The mold is white in color when it is young but it may darken with age. It should not show any yellow, black, or green splodges. Examples include Brie, Camembert, and Coulommiers.

WASHED RINDS These rinds have a characteristic orange-red color to them. They are soft and damp to the touch but should not be slimy. The rind is not eaten. Examples include Pont l'Évêque, Taleggio, Livarot, Limburg, and Mahon.

DRY NATURAL RINDS These rinds are formed by the curds at the edges of the cheese drying out. They may be brushed or scraped, bandaged to make them coarse and grainy, or oiled to become smooth and shiny. They are generally tough, hard, and thick, and molds may grow on the coarser ones. They are not usually eaten. Examples include Stilton (brushed),

Cheddar (bandaged), and Emmental (oiled).

ORGANIC RINDS These are added by the cheesemaker and include herbs or leaves. They are often added after the cheese has ripened. Examples include some goat cheese (herbs) and Banon (leaves).

ARTIFICIAL RINDS These, too, are added by the cheesemaker and include ash, wax, and plastic. Examples include some goat cheese (ash), Edam (wax), and some Cheddars (plastic).

Cheesemaking processes

FRESH CHEESE These are cheeses which are not ripened at all or for only a few days. Some may be lightly pressed or molded; others are simply packed into crocks or tubs. Examples include curd cheese, Quark, Mascarpone, Feta, and cream cheese.

UNPRESSED RIPENED CHEESE The curds are cut as little as possible and allowed to drain naturally. They may be quick-ripened with surface molds or bacteria, or slow-ripened with starter cultures for one to three months. Examples include Brie, Camembert, and Pont l'Évêque (surface molds or bacteria), Esrom and Stilton (starter culture).

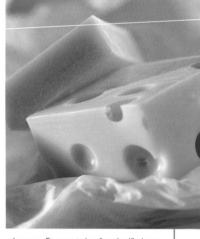

PRESSED RIPENED CHEESE These cheeses are lightly or heavily pressed before ripening for anything from two through eighteen months. Examples include Cheddar, Manchego, and Montasio.

above: *Emmental, a "cooked" cheese.*

COOKED, PRESSED, AND RIPENED CHEESE The curds are heated or "cooked" in the whey before being milled, molded, and heavily pressed. They may be ripened for as long as four years. Examples include Gouda, Parmesan, Gruyère, and Emmental.

PASTA FILATA CHEESE After cooking, the curds are kneaded and stretched before shaping. They may be eaten at once or ripened. Examples include Mozzarella (fresh) and Provolone (ripened).

Appreciating Cheese

In an ideal world everyone would buy enough cheese for their needs that day and buy again the next. To encourage this, specialty cheese shops go to great lengths to bring their cheeses to the peak of condition and maintain them there until they are sold or discarded. Unfortunately most people are unable to shop daily and instead buy food once a week. However, if you want good cheese for entertaining, or simply because you like good cheese, do try to buy it the day you are going to serve it and buy it from an outlet that understands cheese.

So many of the world's great cheeses now have factory versions of the farmhouse originals. These usually do not taste the same so you need to know where the cheese you are buying comes from. Of course, there are exceptions and some mass-produced cheeses are very good indeed. These include certain New Zealand Cheddars and American Provolone cheeses, among others.

Over the years various producing countries have set up denomination of origin systems—AOC in France, for example, and DOC in Italy—which protect the names of their best cheeses. These cheeses must come from specific regions and must be made to traditional recipes. Most of these and more are now also protected under the EU Protected Denomination of Origin (PDO) system for food products. Cheeses which are protected in this way carry appropriate symbols on their labels, so where possible check the whole cheese.

However, it is important to remember that denomination of origin systems do not guarantee the quality of any given cheese. There will still be good and bad producers and farmhouse dairies and factories. So talk to your cheese supplier and see what he or she has to say about the origins of the cheese in which you are interested. Even if you are buying cheese for cooking, you should still buy a good quality cheese for this will give you the best flavor to your final dish.

You may also see reference to Protected Geographical Indication (PGI) or to Certificate of Specific Character (CSC). Here the geographical link must occur in at least one of the stages of production (PGI) or the product must be prepared according to traditional methods (CSC).

Denomination of Origin Cheeses

Here is a list of all the cheeses listed in the Cheese Directory which have PDO designated status.

*Designates those cheeses which it is illegal to import into the United States.

THE PDO CHEESES OF BELGIUM
Fromage de Herve

THE PDO OR AOP (ORIGINALLY AOC) CHEESES OF FRANCE
Beaufort, Bleu d'Auvergne, Bleu de Gex, Bleu de Causses, Brie de Meaux, Brie de Melun*, Camembert de Normandie*, Cantal, Chabichou du Poitou, Chaource, Comté, Crottin de Chavignol, Epoisse*, Forme d'Ambert, Forme du Cantal, Langres*, Livarot, Maroilles, Munster, Ossau-Iraty-Brebis Pyrénées, Picodon de l'Ardèche*, Pont l'Évêque, Pouligny-Saint-Pierre, Reblochon, Roquefort, Saint-Nectaire, Sainte-Maure de Touraine, Selles-sur-Cher, Vacherin Mont d'Or*

THE PDO CHEESES OF GREECE
Feta, Kefalograviera

THE PDO OR DOP (ORIGINALLY DOC) CHEESES OF ITALY
Asiago, Caciocavella, Fontina, Gorgonzola, Grana Padano, Mozzarella di Bufala, Parmigiano-Reggiano, Pecorino Romano, Pecorino Sardo, Pecorino Siciliano, Pecorino Toscano, Provolone, Robiola di Roccaverano, Taleggio

THE PDO OR AOP CHEESES OF THE NETHERLANDS
Noor-Hollandse Edam, Gouda

THE PDO OR DOP (ORIGINALLY DO) CHEESES OF SPAIN
Cabrales, Idiazabel, Mahon, Manchego, Picon

THE NAME-CONTROLLED CHEESES OF SWITZERLAND
Appenzell, Emmental, Gruyère, Sbrinz, Raclette, Sapsago, Swiss Tilsit, Tête de Moine, Vacherin Fribourgeois

THE PDO CHEESES OF THE UK
Bonchester, Single Gloucester, Swaledale, Blue Stilton, West Country Farmhouse Cheddar, White Stilton

The next step is to use your eyes and your nose to judge the condition of the cheese. Cheese should smell good. Cheese which smells strongly of ammonia is overripe. Of course, some people like a really smelly Camembert even if it is overripe. Washed rind cheeses have a very strong farmyardlike aroma but this is perfectly normal for these cheeses. They rarely taste as strong when the rind is removed.

If you like pungent cheese, look out for these French varieties: Epoisse, Maroilles, Münster, Langres, Livarot, Camembert, Chaumes.

Cheese should also look good. It should not be beaded with sweat, nor show blobs of fat. Nor should it be very tight and closed looking. All these are the result of bad handling and overheating or overchilling. Any cut surfaces should have a fresh look. Hard cracked

above: *Camembert.*

surfaces or surface mold are usually an indication that the cheese has been left uncut and uncovered for a day or so.

Very mature cheeses may start to wrinkle and shrivel up. Unless you like the smell of ammonia these cheeses are usually best avoided. It is a mistake to assume that the oldest cheeses have the best flavor. Like wine, every cheese has an ideal age when it has reached its peak and tastes best. After that the cheese will start to go downhill.

If you get the chance to taste, start by thinking about the style of the cheese. Is it fresh and sweet, or more mature and tangy? Is it rich and creamy, or firm and springy, and how salty is it? You should also consider the individual taste characteristics of the cheese, remembering that very firm or rubbery cheeses may take more chewing before they develop their full flavor.

The taste spectrum of cheese is very wide and you may encounter all kinds of flavors. Common descriptive words include buttery, milky, creamy, nutty, mushroomy, or even lemony. Other flavors are reminiscent of condensed milk, fudge, fresh almonds, wet vegetation, and many more. The main criterion here is, do you actually like it?

Most good cheeses have a season when they are at their very best. This has to do with the availability of the milk, the growth of good rich pasture, and the optimum ripening period for the cheese. Generally speaking the best milk is produced from animals grazing in the summer and early fall when the grasses, flowers, and clover are at their most lush. How long the cheese is aged after this will determine the optimum time to buy it. Thus Brie de Meaux cheese made from unpasteurized milk takes only one or two months to ripen and will be at its peak in September, October, and early November. Alpine cheeses like Gruyère and Comté, on the other hand, are matured for four or five months so are best bought in January or February.

Serving Cheese

Cheese really can be served at any meal. In Europe the tradition has been to serve the cheese as a separate course at the end of the meal but there is no reason why cheese should not be the meal itself. In Switzerland and The Netherlands cheese is served at breakfast, and in Spain and Greece it often forms part of the *tapas* or *meze* served before or at the start of the meal. A slice of cheese and an apple makes a great snack at any time of the day.

above: *Select a range of cheeses to please every palate for a lunch or dinner party.*

The cheese course is often part of a formal dinner and the question arises of whether to serve it before or after the dessert. In Britain the tradition was to serve cheese at the end of the meal. This was partly because sweet port wine was the usual accompaniment and partly because early medics believed that cheese "closed the stomach." In the rest of Continental Europe the cheese is served after the main course and before the dessert. This allows red wine to be served with the cheese without having the sweetness of the dessert spoil the palate.

Always serve cheese at room temperature. Never take it straight from the refrigerator. There are those who say you should not put cheese in the refrigerator at all, but unless you have a cellar or an old-fashioned larder this is difficult to avoid. If the cheese has come from the fridge, allow it plenty of time to warm up. This may take an hour or even longer for a large wedge of hard cheese depending on the ambient temperature.

above: *From top to bottom, a cheese slicer and a cheese knife.*

There is an art to cutting cheese and the right utensils are a great help here. A cheese wire produces a clean edge and is often used for cutting cheeses in specialty cheese shops. It is possible to buy small ones for use at home.

Special cheese knives come in all shapes and sizes, usually with a serrated edge and a curved and forked tip to pierce the pieces of cut cheese. The best type is ample in size with large holes cut out of the blade. This design allows the knife to cut through large soft cheeses without squashing the paste and it will also deal with crumbly cheeses better than most. A handheld cheese slicer is ideal for slicing semihard cheese thin.

The shape of the cheese should determine the way it is cut. Small round cheeses, such as Banon, should be cut in half. However, do not cut round or square soft cheeses across the center. These should be cut like a cake into triangles. Pyramid shaped cheeses and logs should be sliced. Small and large drum-shaped cheeses should be cut into discs and then wedges like a cake. This is the correct way to cut a Stilton cheese but the old-fashioned way of cutting off the top and spooning out the cheese from the center still has a strong following.

above: *A small, round soft cheese, cut like a cake.*

All wedges, whether they are cut in the shop or at home, should subsequently be cut in such a way that everyone gets a slice with both the center and the outside of the cheese.

Grainy cheeses like Parmesan and Grana Padano are not cut with a knife at all. Instead they are gouged out with a special wide-bladed tool which helps the cheese to break off into natural chunks.

The choice of bread or crackers to go with the cheese will probably depend upon when it is being served. The cheese should be the star of the cheese course and so a good quality plain water biscuit is one of the best accompaniments. Crackers, oatcakes, and wheaten crackers are also very good.

Plowman's Lunches

Here are some ideas for more unusual versions of this British classic. Serve with plenty of your favorite bread.

English Cheddar with grainy mustard and fresh bananas
Scottish Caboc with oatcakes and loganberries
New Zealand vintage mature Cheddar with fresh apples and cranberry sauce
Double Gloucester with olives and sun-dried tomato paste
Danish Blue with grapes and fresh walnuts (see right)
Stilton with mango chutney, celery, and watercress

Bread is the ideal choice for a plowman's or cheese buffet. Serve a good crusty bread or leave the choice to the diners with a mixture of differently textured breads, such as whole-wheat bread or a baguette. It is also fun to match the style of the bread to the nationality of the cheese. Thus you might serve ciabatta or focaccia with Italian cheeses, baguettes with French cheeses, and landbrot or pumpernickel with German cheeses.

Celery, grapes, and apples are often served with cheese but all kinds of raw fruit or vegetables go well with cheese. Serve pears with Gorgonzola, walnuts with Roquefort, caraway seeds with Münster, and freshly shelled fava beans with Pecorino cheese—a Tuscan specialty in the early summer. In Yorkshire in the north of England, Wensleydale cheese is often served with fruit cake or apple pie or used in the pastry.

The Cheese Board

It is tempting to rush out and buy a whole range of interesting-looking cheeses for a cheese and wine buffet or a celebration cheese board. But once home, you may find that the selection does not look quite so good. A few carefully chosen cheeses may well complement each other far better than a haphazard array. Indeed one large cheese, in first-class condition, could be an even better choice at the end of a meal.

Whether you have a selection of cheeses or a single cheese, it is a good idea to consider the preceding courses. Rich or complex cheeses are best served after plain roasted and broiled meats whereas hard goat cheese and the traditional English cheeses are a good choice to follow more opulent dishes. Young and refreshing cheeses do well after spicy food.

Color, texture, pungency, and flavor all play a part on a well-balanced cheese board. A selection of cheeses which looks very similar in color and texture is not as attractive as one which offers variety. Resist the temptation to include only your favorite styles of cheese; not everyone wants to stick to soft mild cheeses or likes pungent washed-rind ones.

Unless you are serving a cheese buffet, avoid placing the cheeses on a board that is too large or too heavy to pass round. Have more than one cheese knife to hand, particularly if there are some soft-paste cheeses which are likely to stick to the blade.

Alternatively, precut the cheese and serve each guest with a plate containing a small sample of each cheese. This method of serving cheese has been gaining ground in restaurants which are too mean to maintain a cheese board or trolley. The disadvantage is that everyone has to have the same cheese even if they would prefer to chose only one or two of their own favorites.

Suggested Tasting Boards

You can have a lot of fun, with a group of friends, tasting cheeses from around the world. Start by comparing and contrasting the cheeses of each producing country and then move on to make up your own favorite cheese boards.

CLASSIC FRENCH TASTING BOARD
Comté, Brie de Meaux, Chèvre Log, Pont l'Évêque, Roquefort

ADVENTUROUS FRENCH TASTING BOARD
Bleu d'Auvergne, Valency, Explorateur, Epoisse, Tomme de Savoie, Banon

SWISS TASTING BOARD
Appenzell, Emmental, Sapsago, Tête de Moine, Vacherin Mont d'Or

ITALIAN TASTING BOARD
Fontina d'Aosta, Gorgonzola, Parmigiano-Reggiano, Robiola, Taleggio

CLASSIC ENGLISH TASTING BOARD
Duckett's Caerphilly, Farmhouse Lancashire, Mature Cheddar, Stilton, Wensleydale

NEW BRITISH FARMHOUSE CHEESE TASTING BOARD
Cotherstone, Milleens, Ragstone, Sharpham, Ticklemore

AMERICAN CHEESE BOARD
Capriole Banon, Maytag Blue, Shelburne Farm's Raw-milk Cheddar, Vella's Bear Flag Dry Jack

above: *An adventurous French tasting board.*

A cheese buffet, on the other hand, calls for a more imaginative presentation. Ideas include marble slabs, ceramic tiles, or wicker trays in place of the traditional board. Decorate with fresh herbs, wild flowers, salad leaves, summer berries, vegetable flowers, vine leaves, nuts, or dried flowers.

Cover prepared cheese boards with plastic wrap, aluminum foil, or a glass dome and the cheese will remain fresh for an hour or two. If the cheese is to remain under a globe for a longer period, add a cube of sugar to absorb the moisture which will evaporate from the cheese. For longer-term storage of cheese, place in the warmest section of the refrigerator. These include the door sections and the salad crisper. The domestic refrigerator is really set at too cold a temperature for most cheese. The ideal would be a pantry or cellar with a temperature of around 50°F.

Protect the cheese by wrapping in aluminum foil or wax paper, or place in a plastic box with a tight-fitting lid. All these methods will allow the cheese to breathe and, if necessary, develop a little. Plastic wrap is useful for very short-term storage of most cheeses. But do not leave for too long or the rind will start to go slimy and the paste may sweat. Make sure the wrapping is pressed against the cut side of a soft cheese as this will help

above: *Wax paper used to wrap cheese ready for storing.*

to stop it running. Do not wrap more than one piece of cheese in the same wrapping or their flavors will mingle.

If you have a storage place at the correct temperature, cover any cut surfaces closely with wax paper and wrap in cheesecloth or a clean dish towel or more paper. Soft cheeses can be stored in their original boxes but in new wrappings. Most homes are too dry to store cheese well but if you have a whole cheese to store it can help to keep it, well wrapped, inside a cardboard box.

Storage times can vary depending on the type of cheese. Soft cheeses do not keep well, but semihard and hard cheeses can be kept for a while. It is certainly worth buying a large piece of Emmental or Parmesan. Cut it into usable size pieces before storing so that you do not have to bring too much of the cheese up to room temperature before use. Parmesan will keep for many weeks in the domestic refrigerator. Freezing cheese does it no good at all. Soft cheese loses its flavor and hard cheese goes crumbly.

Do not throw away cheese which you have kept for too long or have kept in the wrong conditions. Wipe the droplets of fat off sweating cheese or cut off a thin slice to expose the cleaner cheese inside. If it is too dry, shred it and use on toast or in cooked dishes. Some hard cheeses can be softened for cooking by leaving them for a short period wrapped in a cloth soaked in white wine.

Wine and Cheese

Cheese seems to have a particular affinity with wine and the two tastes can really complement each other. There are two schools of thought here; those who suggest that you should simply drink your favorite wine with your cheese and enjoy it, and those who believe

that some wine and cheese combinations really do not work and that you should plan the match with care. In practice, the former view is more likely to dominate but if you have the time you really can add to your enjoyment of cheese by finding the best partnerships.

Traditionally red wine was considered to be the best match for cheese and this is very often the case. However, white wines and indeed sweet white wines can be even better. Start by choosing wine and cheese of the same general character. A young fresh wine like Beaujolais will go well with a similarly young and fresh cheese, such as Pecorino Fresco or a small Banon. However a mature Barolo would be the better choice for an aged Provolone. A full-bodied and well-flavored wine like Rioja or Australian Shiraz is also needed to

above: *Cabrales with red wine.*

partner strong cheeses like Maroilles and Gaperon and Cabrales. Both the acidity and the tannin levels of the wine affect any partnership of wine and cheese. Wines with high acidity work well with soft creamy cheeses whereas the same cheeses can make tannic wines seem very dry. Cheddar, on the other hand, is very tolerant of tannin in wine. Remember, though, that wine and cheese are not static products. They both change over time and a wine which matches a young Cheddar may not be the best choice for an 18-month-old cheese.

Very often partnerships are suggested by the region from which the cheese comes. Wines from the same region have an immediate affinity. Some of these point the way to white wine and cheese combinations such as Sancerre with the small goat cheeses of the upper Loire and Alsace Gewürztraminer with Münster.

Sweet white wines come into their own with some of the blue cheeses. In France, the favorite choice to accompany Roquefort is Sauternes and, the traditional accompaniment to Stilton is Port.

Cooking with Cheese

Some cheese, such as Gruyère, Parmesan, and Mozzarella, are particularly associated with cooking. This is because they have an excellent flavor or because they produce the kind of texture required by the cook. However, other cheeses which have not been traditionally associated with cooking, such as blue cheese and goat cheese, can also give very good results.

above: *Quick Bean Pot with Cheddar Topping.*

The secret of cooking with cheese is not to overcook it. Where possible cook it slowly or add it toward the end of the cooking time. Over a certain temperature, the protein (casein) in the cheese coagulates and separates out to form a tough, stringy mass. This

above: *Turkey Burgers with Blue Cheese Sauce.*

tendency is reduced if the cheese is mixed with a starchy food such as flour or bread crumbs. Hard, well-ripened cheeses can tolerate higher temperatures than soft cheese because more of the protein has been changed into less complex substances. Fondue, which is kept bubbling at the table, works because the alcohol in the spirits used to flavor the dish keeps the temperature of the cheese below the point at which the cheese would curdle. All cheeses are easier to incorporate into this and other cooked dishes if they are shredded or cut into small pieces. It is important to take into account the strength, piquancy and flavor as well, when cooking particular dishes. If you are cooking with blue cheese, remember that its flavor intensifies with heat. However, this does not seem to happen to goat cheese which actually loses some of its characteristic mustiness.

Cheese and Nutrition

Cheese is an excellent food which, in recent years, has suffered from a bad press. The problem has been that cheese is seen as being relatively high in fat. It also contains cholesterol. In fact, the fat content of cheese is not nearly as high as many people think and, if eaten in moderation, there is no reason why cheese should not form part of a nutritious and balanced diet. Indeed there are many reasons why it should be included.

Cheese is an important source of calcium and a few ounces of cheese can supply most dietary requirements. Cheese also contains significant amounts of the fat-soluble vitamins A and D as well vitamin B complex and vitamin E. Low-fat cheeses made from skim milk contain less of the fat-soluble vitamins, particularly vitamin A. Sodium and phosphorous are also present in some quantity. Phosphorous works with calcium to build strong bones and teeth, and is vital for energy production.

Cheese is made up of water, fat, and protein. The fat, which includes both saturated fatty acids (about 60 percent) and unsaturated fatty acids, does not make up the major part of the content; water does that. But the percentage fat content of cheese is worked out on the basis of dry weight. Thus the figure of 45 percent fat which is given in the information box for both Camembert and Emmental, for example, refers to fat content of these cheeses after all the water has been removed. This percentage is more accurately referred to as "in dry matter" (IDM) in the US or "matière grasse" (m.g.) in Europe. As a general rule of thumb, the actual butterfat content of a cheese labeled 45 percent IDM or m.g. is found by dividing by two, which in this case gives 22.5 percent fat overall.

However, Emmental has a higher actual fat content ounce for ounce than Camembert. This is because it contains less water. This means that, if eaten in the same quantities, seemingly "creamier" cheeses like Camembert have fewer calories and are less fattening than very firm cheeses such as Emmental.

Cheese makes a very attractive alternative to meat and poultry dishes. Its actual protein content may not be quite as high as those foods but more of the protein that is present is immediately usable by the body—around 70 percent compared with 67 or 68 percent for meat and poultry.

Some people restrict their intake of cheese because they believe that they have an intolerence for lactose. However most of the lactose in milk is removed with the whey during manufacture. As a result of this most ripened cheeses contain 95 percent less lactose than the whole milk from which they were made.

above: *Cheese provides a valuable source of protein and makes a healthy snack served with fruit and nuts.*

part two

The cheese directory

Appenzell	Gruyère
Asiago d'allevo	Gubbeen
Austrian Smoked Cheese	Haloumi
Baby Bel	Havarti
Banon	Idiazabal
Bavarian Blue	Jack
Beaufort	Kefalotiri
Beenleigh Blue	Lanark Blue
Bel Paese	Lancashire
Bleu d'Auvergne	Langres
Bleu de Bresse	Le Brouère
Bleu de Gex Haut Jura	Leicester
Bonchester	Leiden
Boursault	Limburg
Boursin	Livarot
Brie	Mahon
Brillat Savarin	Manchego
Brindamour	Maroille
Cabrales	Maytag
Caerphilly	Milleens
Camembert	Mimolette
Cantal	Morbier
Cashel Blue	Mozzarella
Cave Cheese	Munster
Chabichou de Poitou	Ossau-Iraty-Brebis Pyrénées
Chaource	Parmigiano-Reggiano
Cheddar	Pecorino
Cheshire	Picodon
Chèvre	Pont l'Évêque
Colby	Port Salut
Comté	Provolone
Cornish Yarg	Pyrénées
Coulommiers	Raclette
Cream Cheese	Reblochon
Crottin de Chavignol	Ricotta
Curd or Cottage Cheese	Robiola
Dales Cheeses	Roquefort
Danish Blue	Saint-Maure
Edam	Saint-Nectaire
Emmental	Samsoe
English Hard Goat Cheese	Sapsago or Schabzeiger
Epoisse	Sbrinz
Esrom	Selles-sur-Cher
Explorateur	Shropshire Blue
Feta	Stilton
Fontina	Taleggio
Fourme d'Ambert	Tête de Moine
Gaperon	Tetilla
Gjetost	Tilsit
Gloucester	Tomme d'Aligot
Gorgonzola	Vacherin Fribourgeois
Gouda	Valençay
Grana Padano	Wensleydale

Appenzell

*S*mall family groups used to make this distinctively fruity cheese high in their mountain chalets in the eastern cantons of Switzerland close to Austria. Today, production is also centered on St. Gallen, Thurgau, and Zurich.

Appenzell is a hard mountain cheese which was made to keep through the winter months. It looks a little like Gruyère but is sharper and perhaps more interesting in flavor. It has a characteristic light tan color which comes from continuous brushing with a special mixture of spices, wine, and salt.

The cheeses are made in three-inch thick wheels of varying weight. The paste is a rich buttery color, regularly scattered with little pea-size "eyes." Farm-produced cheeses have quite a number of these eyes but large creamery-made cheeses do not always have so many.

Appenzell has a pungent, farmyardlike aroma and a distinctively fruity taste which lingers for a while on the palate. This is a sophisticated cheese which makes an excellent snack on a cold winter's day. Serve it with crusty whole-wheat bread or sourdough rolls and a good quality sweet butter.

The Swiss slice it thinly with a special handheld cheese slicer and serve it with fresh fruits or salads. They also use it to make well-flavored cheese fritters, frying fancy shapes in a batter of eggs, beer, and milk. It is a very versatile cheese because it also melts well into gratins, sauces, or fondue.

Appenzell is made from unpasteurized whole milk. After curdling with rennet, the curds are cut coarse and cooked gently before being transferred to molds. Then they are placed in cool storage cellars with high humidity and rubbed regularly. They remain there for three to five months, and a little longer for Appenzell Extra.

To be sure of the authenticity of your Appenzell cheese, look out for a rampant bear on the label. This symbol is taken from the arms of the Canton of Appenzell from whence most of the cheeses come.

VARIATION

Rasskass: Made from skim milk and matured for much longer than regular Appenzell, the cheese has a darker color and even sharper taste. It has a special black and gold foil label.

Alte Maa

Known as "Old Man's Bread," this simple dish makes a good supper served with a mixed salad. Layer slices of day-old brown bread in a deep dish with Appenzell cheese and seasoning. Pour a little milk over and let stand for 1 hour until all the milk has been absorbed. Transfer to a frying pan and press down well. Fry on both sides for 5 to 6 minutes until crisp and brown.

milk	Unpasteurized cow's milk
style	Hard, cooked, and pressed, washed rind
fat content	45 %
maturity	3 to 5 months
pungency	Medium to strong
wine	Full-bodied Syrah or Shiraz

Asiago d'allevo

Northeastern Italy

$\mathscr{C}$heese has been made on the high plateau of Asiago in northeastern Italy for a thousand years or more, although sheep not cows were the source of milk in days gone by. Production is now centered on Vicenza and Trento provinces, and parts of Padua and Treviso.

Modern Asiago d'allevo is produced in large flat wheels around 12 to 14½ inches in diameter. It has a grayish-yellow rind and a pale straw-colored paste which is supple but sliceable. There are numerous small eyes. The flavor is attractively nutty with a slightly lemony aftertaste. The paste hardens and the flavor strengthens as the cheese matures and it takes on a more tangy character.

Serve younger cheeses on a cheese board with Italian bread. Shred older cheeses over polenta, pasta, or soup, or stir into the risottos which are so characteristic of the Padua region. You will not need to use a great deal as the flavor is penetrating. Asiago is made from cow's milk which is left to settle for six to twelve hours in small vats and then skimmed. Less frequently the milk from two

above: *Pasta Bake with Grated Asiago.*

separate milkings is used. In this case, only the first is skimmed and so the cheese has a higher fat content.

After heating the milk and draining off the whey, the curds are put into special wooden molds called *fascere* and then into plastic ones where a denomination of origin mark is impressed. The cheeses are then immersed in brine and stored for three to five months in order to ripen.

VARIATIONS

Asiago Vecchio and Stravecchio: These cheeses are matured for nine months and two years respectively. The flavor sharpens and strengthens as the cheese ages.

Asiago Pressato: This is a much more commercial type of Asiago made in lowland creameries and it is widely exported. It is made from pasteurized whole milk and thus has a higher fat content than Asiago d'allevo. It is pressed to speed up the ripening process and then matured for only a very short time. The paste is slightly rubbery with few holes and a very mild flavor.

American Asiago: Good versions of this cheese are made in the United States by the Vella Cheese Company of California and Bel-Gioioso Auricchio Cheese Inc. of Wisconsin. Other American versions of this cheese are more like Provolone than Asiago. Asiago is a fairly new venture for the Vella Cheese Company but the result is rich, fruity, and perhaps a little sweeter than the BelGioioso version. The Vella and BelGioioso cheeses are aged for six to twelve months.

milk	Unpasteurized, low-fat cow's milk
style	Hard, cooked curd, washed rind
fat content	30 %, sometimes 45 % (pressato)
maturity	3 to 5 months
pungency	Medium to strong
wine	Well-flavored Chardonnay

Austrian Smoked Cheese

Austria

$\mathcal{T}$his is a processed cheese which comes in various sizes of sausage-shaped plastic packs. The paste is pale in color and very dense with a rubbery texture. It is made by blending a mixture of young Gruyère and Emmental-type cheeses. Serve as part of a mixed cheese board or on its own with celery and crackers.

VARIATIONS

German Smoked Cheese: This is very similar but the cheeses are smoked after they are processed rather than before and the flavor is often harsher.

Brother Basil: This flatish, mahogany, wax-coated, German cheese is made by traditional methods and then smoked. The yellow paste has small holes and is supple, with a pleasantly smoky flavor.

milk	Pasteurized full-fat cow's milk
style	Semihard, processed with plastic coating
fat content	45 %
maturity	Not applicable
pungency	Mild
wine	Lightly oaked Chardonnay

Baby Bel

France

*T*his rather pretty little wax-covered cheese was invented in France in 1931. The coating enables them to keep for three to four months. Despite its rather bland flavor it has proved extremely popular and the Bel company now has factories in Spain, Algeria, Denmark, and Japan.

Baby Bel is made in much the same way as Edam and has a similar pale paste and firm, almost rubbery, texture. The flavor is perhaps more like a very mild Gouda with a light fudgy taste. It makes a useful snack or picnic cheese.

VARIATION

Albany: Baby Bel is manufactured under licence in Kentucky and sold under the name of Albany.

milk	Cow's milk
style	Semihard, cooked, and pressed, wax wrapped
fat content	45 %
maturity	2 to 3 months
pungency	Very mild
wine	Light Beaujolais-style red

Banon

Southeast France

*T*his delicious little French cheese, named for the market town of Banon in northern Provence, is wrapped in chestnut leaves and tied with raffia. The rind is slightly sticky and may blue with age. The paste is white and slightly crumbly with a faint lactic smell. The flavor is mild with a hint of sourness.

VARIATIONS

Saint-Marcellin: This is made in the Dauphine region of Provence, almost always from cow's milk.

American Banon: Sally Jackson of Washington State makes a small goat's milk cheese, similar to Banon with a complex herby flavor. Judy Schad of Capriole in Indiana also makes a goat's milk Banon, macerated in white wine and brandy.

milk	Ewe's, goat's, or cow's milk
style	Soft, natural rind
fat content	45 %
maturity	2 weeks to 2 months
pungency	Mild to strong
wine	Pinot Blanc

Bavarian Blue

Bavaria, Germany

*T*his highly successful cheese is a modern hybrid. It combines the white mold rind of a Camembert with the blue veins of a Gorgonzola. Indeed, the best-known brand, Cambozola, takes its name from these two cheeses.

The paste is creamy white in color with patches, rather than veins, of pale blue mold. The flavor is very mild and gentle with just a hint of mushrooms and lemons. Remove from the refrigerator at least an hour before serving. Serve on sandwiches or in soups.

milk	Pasteurized cow's milk with cream
style	Semisoft, white mold rind, blue veined
fat content	70 %
maturity	2 to 4 weeks
pungency	Mild and gentle, rather boring
wine	Dry Riesling wines

VARIATIONS

Bla Castello: This is the Danish version of this cheese.
Timboon Farmhouse Blue: An Australian soft rind blue cheese made with organic milk by Timboon Farmhouse Cheeses in Victoria.

Beaufort

Haute-Savoie, France

*T*his is France's splendid answer to Gruyère. Its darkly rich flavor is the result of ripening in the cool and humid caves and cellars of the Haute-Savoie mountains. The village of Beaufort is situated in a remote part of the region. Here Tarentaise cattle graze the lush Alpine meadows to give a milk which is full of flavor.

The cheeses themselves are made in large cylinder shapes with quite tall concave sides. They may weigh as much as 88 lb. Each cheese has a natural, thin, dark yellow, almost burnt ocher, rind. The paste is smooth and very firm but supple with few holes or cracks, although there may be the occasional horizontal fissure.

The paste smells of nuts and toffee and the taste is very distinctive. There are unusual nutty, mellow caramel flavors and not too much salt. It is a cheese to love or hate. Serve good chunks of it with crusty baguettes and sweet butter on an outdoor picnic or

milk	Unpasteurized cow's milk
style	Hard, cooked curd, pressed, natural brushed rind
fat content	50 %
maturity	Minimum 6 months up to 2 years
pungency	Medium
wine	Lightly oaked Chardonnay

pack it with a mixed salad for a delicious desktop lunch. If you prefer to serve it at the end of the meal, let it shine by serving it on its own with plain crackers and perhaps an almond or two.

Beaufort is a versatile cheese which can be used in any number of ways. The locals use it in the traditional *Omelette à la Savoyarde* and in gratin potatoes with butter and milk. Indeed it is a particularly good cheese for cooking as it melts so beautifully. Try it melted over charbroiled zucchini or in baked potatoes.

The cheese is made in high mountain chalets in a similar way to Emmental and Gruyère. The best cheeses are made in August from the late summer milk and these start to appear in the shops in March or April. However, some of the best Beaufort is matured for more than the minimum five months and so could come onto the market at any time. Some cheeses made from the late summer milk are labeled Beaufort d'Alpage. If they are they will almost certainly cost more.

Omelette à la Savoyarde

Slice 4 medium-size boiled potatoes and fry in butter until very lightly browned. Mix 8 eggs with 1 cup shredded Beaufort cheese. Season and pour over the fried potatoes. Cook until the base is set. Finish off under a hot broiler. If you like, you can add some chopped fresh chervil, or your favorite fresh herb, to the mix but this is not traditional.

RECIPE

Beenleigh Blue

$\mathcal{T}$he green valleys of Devon are home to this well-flavored blue cheese made from unpasteurized ewe's milk. Robin and Sari Congdon started limited production in Totnes in the 1980s. Today they are able to produce enough cheese to sell it all year round. They also produce blue cheeses from cow's and goat's milk.

The cheese has a very thin natural rind and comes wrapped in foil. The blue veins form an uneven, rather patchy, pattern mainly in the slightly crumbly paste. The aroma is full of toasty nuts and mold. The strong flavor hits the palate with upfront fruitiness, wine, and nuts, fading through a sweet and creamy mellow stage to a mushroomy finish which is rather a surprise after the attack at the beginning.

Serve as a cheese course with Port or dessert wine and plain crackers, either on its own or with a selection of other hard and soft cheeses. Or use to make salad dressings, blue cheese pizza, or sprinkle on broiled goat cheese with pine nuts as an appetizer.

right: *Broccoli Pizza topped with Blue Cheese.*

Harbourne Blue: This is a handmade blue cheese made with unpasteurized goat's milk. The goats graze on the edge of Dartmoor in Devon and produce a very aromatic milk. The cheese is semihard in style and matured for three months to give a very aromatic and distinctive flavor.

Devon Blue: This blue cheese is now made with cow's milk from a number of farms and as a result Roger Congdon has decided to heat treat the milk gently but it has not affected the flavor too much. The cheese, which is matured for six months, is wrapped in gold foil. It has a leafy moldy aroma with nuts and raisins, and a deliciously lingering creamy flavor with roasted nuts and soft leather.

Beet Soup with Beenleigh Blue

Chop 2 onions and gently sauté in butter until opaque. Add 9 oz peeled and chopped beet, a large peeled and chopped potato, 3½ cups broth, and seasoning. Bring to a boil, cover, and simmer until the beet is cooked through. Purée in a blender then return to the pan and reheat. Cut a baguette into rounds and toast well. Press on plenty of Beenleigh Blue and pop under the broiler. Ladle the soup into bowls and top with the Beenleigh Blue croûtons.

RECIPE

milk	Sheep's milk
style	Soft blue
fat content	47 %
maturity	5 to 8 months
pungency	Medium
wine	Port

Bel Paese

Northern Italy

*T*his bland cheese was created by the Galbani cheese family in the early part of the twentieth century. It has proved extremely popular, particularly in the United States. It is now made in large factories in Lombardy in Italy and in New Jersey.

Bel Paese is made in smallish discs with a thin shiny rind. The paste is a pale creamy yellow with a few small holes. It is too firm to spread but a little too soft to slice well. It has a milky, buttery aroma and a gently buttery flavor with a slight tang to it. It is useful in cooking as it melts well without becoming tough.

milk	Pasteurized cow's milk
style	Semihard, uncooked, pressed, washed rind
fat content	45 to 52 %
maturity	6 to 8 weeks
pungency	Very mild
wine	Light Chardonnay or Barbera

VARIATION

Italico: This is the name given to a range of very similar cheeses sold under different brand names and made by Galbani's competitors.

Bleu d'Auvergne

Auvergne, France

$\mathcal{B}$leu d'Auvergne started life as an imitation of Roquefort, using cow's milk in place of ewe's milk. It is now made in the Cantal and Puy-de-Dome regions of the Massif Central and has established itself as a first-class name-designated cheese in its own right. Bleu d'Auvergne was originally made on the local farms and a small amount still is, but the vast majority of cheeses are now creamery made. Like Roquefort, the cheeses were traditionally matured in humid cellars and pierced with needles after two months.

It is produced in medium-size flat cylinders. The rind is very thin and so the cheese is usually wrapped in foil. The paste is very rich and creamy with a pretty pale yellow color, darkening a little near the rind. There are a few holes scattered through the paste and well-defined, and well-distributed, greenish-blue veining.

milk	Pasteurized cow's milk
style	Semihard, blue veined, salty rind
fat content	45 %
maturity	About 3 months
pungency	Medium with good piquancy
wine	Sauternes

The cheese has a wonderful aroma of freshly baked cream crackers. The taste is rich and full with a light saltiness which increases with the incidence of veining. The overall flavor is piquant but not oversharp. Serve as an after-dinner cheese with sweet grapes.

Bleu d'Auvergne is a good cheese to cook with because it melts beautifully. Use it sparingly to flavor soufflés or, more unusually, soufflé omelets. Cut into mixed leaf salads or blend into dressings for fine beans and walnuts or salad potatoes. If you are storing Bleu d'Auvergne for any period of time, remove its own foil covering and double wrap in fresh foil.

VARIATIONS

Bleu des Causses: Strictly speaking this is not a variation but another AOC cheese in its own right. However it does come from the Massif Central and it is very similar to Bleu d'Auvergne. Made in Rouergue in Aquitaine from unpasteurized milk, it is matured in caves similar to those at Combalou where Roquefort is matured. It has an even creamier texture than Bleu d'Auvergne and a slightly more complex flavor.

Bleu de Quercy: This is very similar to Bleu des Causses.

Blue Cheese and Cauliflower Soup

Chop 2 leeks and gently fry in butter to soften then add a small glass of sherry, a small cauliflower cut into pieces, and 3 cups vegetable broth. Bring to a boil, cover, and simmer for 20 minutes. Purée the mixture and stir in 3½ oz crumbled Bleu d'Auvergne. Gently reheat and serve at once.

RECIPE

Bleu de Bresse

Burgundy, France

*B*leu de Bresse was invented in 1950 by the cheesemakers of northeastern France as a smaller and more marketable version of Saingorlon, which itself was a First World War copy of Gorgonzola. It is now all factory-made from pasteurized milk.

The cheese comes in various sizes, all with a smooth, off-white to bluish rind. The paste is pale and creamy with patches of greenish-blue veining. There is a light milky aroma and a mild mushroomy flavor. Slice small cheeses into salads with toasted pine nuts or serve on a cheese board with celery or pears.

VARIATION

Pipo Crème: This is just one of the various brand names used by French creameries.

milk	Pasteurized cow's milk
style	Soft, blue-veined, mold rind
fat content	50 %
maturity	A few weeks
pungency	Mild
wine	Light to medium reds like Fleurie

Bleu de Gex Haut Jura

Northeast France

*B*leu de Gex and its very near neighbor and cousin Bleu de Septmoncel are grouped together under the PDO designation of Bleu de Gex Haut Jura. However, most cheese-mongers sell these cheeses under their own names even though they are very similar.

Made in wheels weighing up to 15 lb, Bleu de Gex Haut Jura cheeses have a natural brushed rind which is dry, rough, and whitish yellow in color. Avoid any cheeses which are cracked or slimy to the touch. The paste is dense and creamy with a pale ivory color and a marbling of very dark greenish-blue veins. The aroma and flavor are relatively mild but quite definite in character. The taste is quite sharp and bitter.

Serve as a lunchtime snack with pickled walnuts and celery, or cream into a dressing for a mixed-leaf salad with walnuts.

milk	Unpasteurized cow's milk
style	Soft blue, natural brushed rind
fat content	45 %
maturity	2 to 3 months
pungency	Medium
wine	Good white Burgundy

Bonchester

Scotland

$\mathcal{T}$his well-flavored soft cheese from the Scottish borders is one of the few British cheeses to qualify for the European Union designation of protected origin (PDO). It is made every day by John and Christian Curtis on their farm at Bonchester Bridge.

It is made in a small, round, shallow disc with a white rind which develops a few freckles. The paste mellows to a deep primrose yellow color. The mature cheese has a buttery, condensed milk aroma and the flavor has a sweet creamy aftertaste.

V A R I A T I O N

Teviotdale: This is a hard cheese which is made by pressing four Bonchester cheeses together. It ripens in 3 to 4 months to give a firm but soft cheese with a creamy floral flavor.

milk	Unpasteurized Jersey cow's milk
style	Soft, mold rind
fat content	44 %
maturity	10 weeks
pungency	Mild
wine	Claret

Boursault

Northwest France

*O*nce known as "Lucullus," this small triple-cream cheese from Normandy and the Ile de France is an excellent example of good factory-made cheese.

It has a light, bloomy, slightly pinkish rind. The paste is extremely creamy and mildly aromatic. The flavor is lightly nutty and not cloying considering the amount of cream used to make it.

Serve on a cheese board in the classic manner with grapes or celery, or use to enrich cheese soups, fondues, or sauces. Remove the rind and melt into a little chicken broth flavored with fresh herbs to make a quick pasta sauce.

Boursault was the invention of Henri Boursault; however, the company is now owned by Boursin. There is a choice of gold and silver label Boursault. The former has the best flavor because it is made from unpasteurized milk.

milk	Enriched cow's milk
style	Soft, triple cream, bloomy rind
fat content	75 %
maturity	3 to 4 weeks
pungency	Mild and nutty
wine	Rioja

Boursin

Northwest France

This savory little cheese, flavored with garlic and herbs, was one of the first flavored cheeses to become fashionable. It is a triple-cream cheese originally factory made in Normandy.

Made in small or miniature drums, there are four versions of the cheese: garlic and herbs, natural, pepper, and legèr, the last being a low-fat version. They are all reasonably well-flavored.

Serve with fresh baguettes, crispbread, or pumpernickel. Use as canapé toppings or as a stuffing for celery stalks, dates, or tomatoes.

milk	Cow's cream
style	Soft, fresh, triple cream
fat content	70 %
maturity	Fresh
pungency	Mild to medium
wine	Sancerre or Sauvignon Blanc

VARIATIONS

Tartare: This is the brand name of a rival cheese, packed in tubs.
Rondelé and Alouette: These are American brand names for herb- and pepper-flavored cheese spreads similar to Boursin.

Brie

Northwest France

𝓑rie is one of a number of French "kings of cheeses." It is said to have gained this accolade at a cheese contest held by the French statesman Talleyrand to relieve the boredom of the negotiations at the Treaty of Vienna after the Battle of Waterloo in 1815. All thirty representatives presented their own national cheeses but when Talleyrand brought in the Brie de Meaux, it was unanimously declared the best. It is now one of the most imitated cheeses in the world.

The original Brie came from the department of Seine-et-Marne in the Ile de France but today the only authentic representatives are Brie de Meaux and Brie de Melun. They have both always been protected by the French appellation controlée (now PDO) laws. So check the label for the designation to see that you are not buying one of the many imitations.

Brie de Meaux is made in flattened discs weighing 2 to 7 lb each. It has a white rind with a pinkish-beige mottling which distinguishes it from many of its copies. The paste has a glossy straw color which deepens to warm ivory and which at its peak should bulge but not run. Avoid cheeses with a very chalky paste. This cheese should have an aroma of farmyards and roasted nuts and just a hint, perhaps, of ammonia. *Laitier* or factory-made cheeses will be milder with simple mushroom aromas. The taste of the farmhouse cheese is very complex with a nutty, fruity flavor. Brie de Melun is slightly smaller and matured for longer than Brie de Meaux.

VARIATIONS

Brie de Melun Affine: This is mature Brie de Melun.

Brie de Melun Frais: This is very young Brie de Melun. It may have no rind at all or it may be coated with ash. The latter are sometimes referred to as "Bleu."

Brie de Montereau: This is a very similar cheese to Brie de Melun Affine, but is only matured for six weeks.

Brie Laitier and French factory-made Brie-style cheeses: Factory-made Brie is produced in a variety of ways but always from pasteurized milk. Unfortunately most *laitier* Brie does not reach anywhere near the heights of the two PDO cheeses. You will find a lightly mushroomy aroma coming from the rind but the paste itself often has very little taste. The texture too can be disappointing. The reason for this is partly that many of the factory cheeses are made to 52 % or even 60 % fat content and partly that they are "stabilized" during their manufacture. This means that they have a uniform texture which does not develop in the way that the *fermier* cheeses develop. They can sit on the supermarket shelf unchanged for months. Brand names include Belle des Champs, Suprême des Ducs, and Délice.

Dunbarra: This is an Irish soft cheese with a white rind and a creamy texture. It is firmer than Brie and milder.

Somerset Brie: This gentle English version of Brie is made in Somerset. It can develop quite a good flavor.

Bath Soft Cheese: This cheese is made to an original nineteenth-century recipe but the end result is very similar to Brie. Made by Grahame Padfield from the raw milk of his own herd, this cheese has full flavor with light mushrooms and a lemony tang.

Vermont Farmhouse Brie: Cheesemakers Karen Galayda and Tom Gilbert, working at the Craigston Cheese Company in Massachusetts, were the very first to make mold-ripened cheeses in the United States. They have now set up their own operation at Blythedale Farm in Vermont where they use a very gentle process to pasteurize the milk so that the resulting cheese has the same type of flavor that you might expect from raw milk.

Fairview Estate Brie: Graham Sutherland produces a Brie-style cheese from a herd of Jersey cows in Suider Paarl, South Africa.

Timboon: This is a prize-winning Australian Brie made from organic milk by Timboon Farmhouse Cheeses in Victoria.

Grape Vine Ash Brie: Made by Peter Curtis at the Hunter Valley Cheese Company in New South Wales. The curd is covered in vine ash and left to mature until the white mold growth covers the ash.

Non-French factory-made Brie-style cheese: This is now made in a variety of countries, often in factories owned by the French creameries. The results are identical to French-produced factory cheese. Some factory-made Brie is also sold under brand names such as Dania from Denmark.

French and German Blue Brie: The Germans invented a blue cheese similar to Brie which was then copied by the French. This cheese has a high fat content because the milk used to make it is enriched with cream.

Abbey Blue Brie: This is an Irish farmhouse cheese made in County Laois from full-fat cow's milk.

milk	Cow's milk
style	Soft, bloomy rind
fat content	45 to 60 %
maturity	Farmhouse cheeses: 4 to 10 weeks, factory cheeses: 3 weeks
pungency	Mild to full and fruity
wine	Full-bodied Chardonnay or German dessert wines

It has a very darkly mottled rind with only traces of white. The paste is golden yellow in color. Aroma and flavor are both much stronger and more rustic than Brie de Meaux.

Brie de Meaux and Brie de Melun deserve to be served on their own. Buy a whole cheese for a dinner or buffet party and leave it to dominate the cheese course. Simply add water biscuits and grapes to accompany it. These cheeses are also very good served on a French plowman's platter with baguettes and sweet pickles, for a light lunch.

A ripe cheese will only keep for about three days if left out. If storing a cut piece, it is a good idea to place a piece of cardboard against the cut edges to prevent the cheese running. Store in a cool place or the salad compartment of the refrigerator.

Brie is a useful cheese for cooking. Remove the rind and the cheese will melt easily into soups and sauces. Try layering it in potato bakes, fish pies, and vegetable casseroles. Cut into wedges and serve on salad leaves with a mustard dressing or coat with egg and bread crumbs and deep fry.

above: *Deep-fried Brie.*

Traditional Brie can be made from both unpasteurized and pasteurized milk. The curds are neither cut nor pressed. The skill lies in the even spooning of layers of curd into cheese rings and the removing of the whey. It is all too easy to make a dry chalky cheese. Once formed the cheeses are placed on straw mats and turned regularly. After a week they are sprinkled with a special Penicillium mold and matured at a carefully controlled temperature until they are ripe. Farmhouse Brie is at its best if bought and eaten in the late summer and fall.

Brillat Savarin

Normandy, France

*T*his amazingly creamy cheese is named for the man who said "a meal without cheese is like a beautiful woman with only one eye." Brillat Savarin, a writer, statesman, and gourmand fled France in Napoleonic times and lived for a while in Virginia.

But the cheese is not as old as its name. It was invented and named earlier this century by Henri Androuet, the legendary Parisian master cheesemonger. It is made in smallish 1 lb deep discs. It has a light downy white rind and a paste which cuts like butter.

Brillat Savarin has a really milky aroma with light lemon sour tones. The flavor is similar but with a meadowsweet creaminess which is most attractive. The adage for this cheese is "the younger the better." If allowed to mature for too long, the rind darkens and the paste becomes unpleasantly oily. Serve after plain broiled meat with a mixed fruit platter of apricots, kiwi fruit, or berries.

milk	Cow's milk enriched with hot cream
style	Very soft, triple cream, bloomy rind
fat content	78 %
maturity	3 weeks
pungency	Very mild
wine	Champagne or Californian sparkling wine

Bridamour

Corsica, France

*T*his is the cheese for those who like herbs. Aromatic Mediterranean herbs, such as rosemary, wild thyme, and savory, are mixed with coriander seeds, juniper berries, and tiny red chillies to form a hedgehog coating on this little round or square cheese. The cheese is also known as Fleur de Maquis.

The young cheese offers a snow-white paste which is creamy, soft, and moist. As the cheese matures, the paste takes on a darker color and starts to run. Eventually the paste will harden again. The pure taste of the young cheese is quite mild and gentle but the herbs on the outside really do flavor the inside. In older cheeses the flavor is much more nutty with a lightly musty tang. Cheeses over two months old have the most concentrated flavor of all.

Serve on a cheese board or cut into cubes and serve with olives as an appetizer or use in salads for lunches and suppers.

milk	Sheep's or goat's milk, or a mixture of the two
style	Soft to hard, rindless, herb coated
fat content	45 %
maturity	2 to 10 weeks
pungency	Mild to medium strong
wine	Gutsy Provence red

Cabrales

Northern Spain

$\mathcal{T}$his is a blue cheese of great character. It is handmade on farms in the Picos de Europa mountains of northern Spain and matured in caves which are aired by cold, damp, and salty winds blowing up from the Bay of Biscay.

The people of Concejo de Cabrales keep cows, goats, and sheep, and use the raw milk of all three in their cheeses, the proportions varying according to availability. The cheese is made in small to medium-size drums with a dark yellow ocher rind which is quite sticky to the touch.

Authentic Cabrales are wrapped in leaves, but the demands of modern health regulations mean that green foil or plastic is more commonly used to wrap the cheese or may even be substituted for the leaves. Avoid the latter if possible as the leaves do give a distinctive flavor to the cheese.

milk	Unpasteurized goats, sheep's, and cow's milk
style	Semihard, matured, natural rind, blue veined
fat content	45 to 48 %
maturity	3 to 6 months
pungency	Strong
wine	Oloroso sherry or Rioja (oaked white or young red)

The paste is creamy white with intensely blue veining which is often more concentrated at the edges of the cheese than in the center. You can almost see the curds and the cheese is so soft that it can be spread on chunks of bread or toast, but it is more crumbly than wet.

The cheese has a strong aroma and a lovely salty tang that really bites the tongue. It also has a robust flavor of lingering complexity with woody, lemony tones. Serve by itself on a cheese board at the end of a good meal or eat as a meal in its own right in the middle of the day with large beefsteak tomatoes and country-style bread. The Spanish mix it with minced black olives to spread on toast or use it in a fonduelike dish made by beating it with hard cider. They also consider it a particularly good cheese for sauces for meat and vegetable dishes.

Buy the best cheeses in the late spring when milk is available from animals which have been grazing on the highland pastures. The locals say that cow's milk acidifies the cheese, goat's milk gives it its piquancy, and sheep's milk gives it its aroma and buttery texture. At other times of the year there may only be small quantities of goat's or sheep's milk, or even none at all.

The cheeses are made by coagulating the mixed milks in the usual way. After several hours curds are irregularly cut into

above: *The Asturias, home to Cabrales and its variations.*

walnut-size pieces and these are then packed into cylindrical molds to drain. Dry-salting is followed by a further drying-out period, after which the cheeses are taken up to the caves. Here mold forms on the outside of the cheese and gradually works its way through the paste. At the same time yeasts form on the outside of the cheese which give the characteristic dark yellow ocher color and the strong smell.

VARIATIONS

Picon: This is a Spanish denomination of origin cheese in its own right but it is very similar indeed to Cabrales. It comes from the other side of the Asturias mountains in Cantabria. Like Cabrales it can be made from cow's, goat's, and sheep's milk but it is more often made from cow's milk alone. Placed side by side with Cabrales, it is very difficult to tell them apart.

Gamonedo or Gamoneu: Like Cabrales, this cheese comes from the Asturias mountains. However, the drum shape is slightly taller and the rind is a grayer color. It is even more strong-smelling. Gamonedo cheeses are gently smoked before maturing in mountain caves. The paste is firmer than Cabrales and has a complex flavor all its own.

Steak with Cabrales Sauce

Soften a large teaspoon of butter in a pan with 7 oz Cabrales cheese over gentle heat. Do not allow the cheese to melt completely. Then add ⅔ cup light cream and stir the mixture until a smooth sauce is formed. Reheat gently when you are ready to use the sauce and pour over four broiled or fried steaks. This sauce works equally well if poured over pasta or potatoe dishes, which could then be baked in the oven to give a crisp topping.

RECIPE

Caerphilly

Wales

*T*he original Caerphilly cheese used to be very popular with Welsh miners who would take it to work and eat it like cake. The cheese is very salty and it must have seemed an ideal way to replenish the salt lost through sweat while working at the coalface. During the Second World War production was stopped as the milk was used to make Cheddar and so the Welsh cheesemakers went out of business.

For many years this Welsh cheese was only made in England, but today it is again made in a small number of farmhouses in the Principality itself. Farms like Caws Cenarth and Glynhynod in Dyfed are now producing first-class farmhouse cheeses.

Shaped like a small millstone, Caerphilly cheese has a very thin rind. The paste is creamy white in color with a moist and crumbly

milk	Cow's milk
style	Semihard, pressed and brined, natural rind
fat content	48 %
maturity	1 to 2 months
pungency	Delicate tangy
wine	Rioja

texture. The flavor of the farmhouse cheese is quite delicate with an attractive lemony acidity and salty quality. Factory-made cheeses rarely capture the subtle quality of this cheese and can be quite bland.

Serve on its own with grapes or apples, or broil on toast with a splash of vinegar. Use with sautéed mushrooms to stuff pancakes.

above: *Stuffed Pancakes with Caerphilly Cheese Sauce.*

The revived farmhouse cheeses are mostly made from unpasteurized milk. They are traditionally lightly pressed and brined for 24 hours before being rubbed with rice flour. Look out for Caerphilly cheeses from Wedmore Farm in Somerset where Chris Duckett makes the wonderfully creamy and well-flavored Duckett's Caerphilly.

VARIATIONS

Wedmore: This is a young Duckett's Caerphilly with a layer of snipped chives which gives its own distinctive flavor to the cheese.
Tournagus: This is Duckett's Caerphilly which has been washed in Kentish wine to give it a slightly sticky red rind and a pungent flavor.
Ribblesdale Goat's Milk: This cheese has an unusually mild flavor for a goat cheese and a texture similar to a young Caerphilly.

RECIPE

Glamorgan Sausages

Mix together equal quantities of fresh bread crumbs, very finely chopped leeks, and shredded Caerphilly cheese. Add chopped fresh parsley, a little mustard powder, and seasoning, and bind with beaten egg. Shape the mixture into small sausage shapes. Roll in flour, then in beaten egg, and then in dried bread crumbs. Fry, turning occasionally, until crisp all over.

Camembert

Northwest France

$\mathcal{O}$ne of the world's most famous cheeses, Camembert originated in the Pays d'Auge in Normandy, but its production is not restricted to France. Indeed it is now made in most countries where cheese is produced on a large scale and is eaten everywhere from San Francisco to Saigon.

The very best cheese is still handmade from raw milk on farms in the original part of Normandy, and this type of Camembert is protected by the French appellation controllée (now PDO) laws. Elsewhere large factories churn out uninteresting cheeses made from pasteurized milk.

"Veritable Camembert de Normandie" is the designation to look out for plus the words "au lait cru" which indicate that unpasteurized milk has been used. These cheeses have a characteristic mold rind with a slight light brown mottling. The pale straw-colored paste should be uniformly ripe, without any chalkiness in the center.

A good cheese has a clean and herby aroma with a good tang of mushrooms. The flavor is creamy and complex with fresh grassy tones. Unless you are addicted to overstrong cheese, avoid those which are so soft that the paste is almost gluey. Camembert is not intended to be so strong that you can smell the ammonia across the room! Check the degree of ripeness by holding the center of the cheese gently between your forefinger and thumb, and press gently. It should yield to the touch but not too much.

One of the best designated cheeses is Isigny Ste. Mere. Unfortunately it is illegal to export this unpasteurized version of Camembert to the United States. The only Camembert available in America is factory produced. Like the farm-made version, it comes in 9 oz discs packed in wafer-thin wooden boxes.

The mold rind often has much more reddish mottling and the paste may well still be chalky. The aroma offers just a touch of mushrooms and the flavor, too, is very mild and not at all complex .

Camembert makes a good snack or plowman's lunch, served with a really fruity pickle. Serve a whole cheese on a cheese buffet or at the end of a meal. Alternatively, take a tip from Timboon Farmhouse Cheeses in Australia and serve with quince paste on rye bread.

It also works very well in the kitchen. Remove the rind and melt into cream sauces for zucchini, pasta (see below), or fish. Mash with chopped nuts or sesame seeds for canapé toppings.

Store Camembert in its box. If it is not fully ripe it can be ripened at home in a cool cupboard. If you put it in the refrigerator it will stop maturing and, of course, will need to be returned to room temperature before serving. Once the cheese is cut, it should be wrapped in foil and eaten as soon as possible.

below: *Ravioli with Camembert Sauce.*

Traditional production is typical of good soft cheesemaking techniques. The milk is gently heated until it is ready for the rennet to be added. Coagulation takes about an hour to an hour and a half. After this time the curds are just about strong enough to go into perforated molds. The cheeses are drained and then sprinkled with the Penicillium mold and dry-salted. They are then ripened in high-humidity cellars.

VARIATIONS

Cooleeney Farmhouse: Made in County Tipperary in Ireland by Jim and Breda Maher, this Camembert-type cheese develops a semi-liquid paste and a strong mushroomy flavor. It is richer and wetter than Camembert. At the time of writing it is still being made from raw milk but sadly Jim Maher feels that he might have to pasteurize in the near future.

Vermont Farmhouse Camembert: Karen Galayda and Tom Gilbert make a very good Camembert-style of cheese at their farm in Corinth. They get round the pasteurization problem by using a very slow and gentle method which does not change the flavor of the milk.

Fairview Estate Camembert: Graham Sutherland produces a Camembert-style cheese from a herd of Jersey cows on the estate in Suider Paarl, South Africa. He also makes St. Martin, a white mold, goat's milk Camembert-style cheese.

Timboon: This is a Camembert-style cheese which is produced from organic milk by Timboon Farmhouse Cheeses in Victoria, Australia.

Top Paddock Camembert: This is another Australian version of this cheese made by Fred Peppin in his small dairy at Bena, Victoria.

milk	Cow's milk
style	Soft, mold rind
fat content	45 to 50 %
maturity	1 to 2 months
pungency	Mild to medium
wine	Normandy or farmhouse hard cider

Cantal

Auvergne, France

Also known as Forme de Cantal, this is one of France's oldest cheeses. The excellence of Cantal was noted by Pliny almost two thousand years ago. It used to be made in the mountain farms of Cantal but today most of it comes from factories in the lowland areas of the region. However, its very close cousin, Salers—named for the local cattle—has remained largely a farmhouse cheese.

Cantal and Salers are both big drum-shaped cheeses weighing as much as 99 lb. They have a thin grayish-beige rind which is dry and powdery and darkens with age. The rind has a tendency to crack, allowing mold to develop in the cheese. Eat or not as you will. The fresh paste is pale yellow in color, close textured, and smooth.

The cheese has a milky aroma and a pleasantly nutty flavor with an attractive lingering acidity to it. A poet once wrote of Cantal that "to elaborate on Cantal is an error of taste; it is all simplicity."

milk	Cow's milk
style	Semihard, pressed, brushed rind
fat content	45 %
maturity	3 to 6 months
pungency	Mild
wine	Rioja

Serve on a French plowman's platter with country-style bread and fresh fruit, or include on a French cheese board. Cantal shreds and melts well and is therefore very useful in cooking. Use it in soups and sauces or to flavor savory choux buns, cheese crackers, or muffins.

right: *Corn Chowder.*

VARIATIONS

Tomme d'Aligot: This is an unripe version of the cheese. It is used to make a local dish, also called Aligot. This is a mixture of mashed potatoes, garlic, bacon, and cheese.

Cantalet: This is a baby, factory-made cheese using pasteurized milk and weighing around 22 lb.

Laguiole: This is another PDO cheese in its own right but the only difference between it and Cantal is that Laguiole is never made with pasteurized milk and it is ripened for longer. The cheese is therefore a little harder and has a much sharper tang to it.

Gratin de Chou

Cantal does not go too stringy and so makes a good choice for gratin recipes. Shred and steam a green or white hearted cabbage and toss in a little cream and seasoning. Place in individual heatproof dishes. Top with shredded Cantal cheese and white bread crumbs mixed in equal quantities. Brown quickly under a hot broiler.

RECIPE

Cashel Blue

Ireland

*L*ouis and Jane Grubb's pedigree herd of Holstein cows grazes the meadows of their farm in County Tipperary and all the milk goes into this small wheel-shaped blue cheese. Each cheese is wrapped in gold foil and carries a batch code number. The first two numbers of the batch correspond to the week of the year so that the age of the cheese is always known.

Cashel Blue has a beige rind, which develops a pinkish cast as it matures, and the paste moves from firm to soft texture. At six weeks of age, when the cheese is first available in the shops, the ivory paste is quite crumbly with a tangy flavor. Over the next six weeks it develops a much creamier texture and a stronger, more piquant flavor of dried herbs and woody leaf mold. For a mature cheese, ripen it at home in your refrigerator at 35 to 43°F. Serve with plain crackers, whole-wheat bread or walnut bread.

milk	Cow's milk
style	Semihard blue cheese
fat content	47 to 54%
maturity	1 to 4 months
pungency	Medium to strong
wine	Light fruity Beaujolais-style wines

Cave Cheese

Northern Denmark

*I*n the early eighties Aage Jensen of the Vellev Dairy near Aarhus in Northern Jutland decided to try using the man-made caves at Monsted to mature some of his cheeses. Their constant temperature and high humidity have proved ideal and his idea has earned the cheese numerous gold medals in Denmark.

Cave cheese is made to a traditional Danbo recipe but modern microfilter equipment allows the milk to be pasteurized at a low temperature and so retain much of its flavor. The cheese is pressed, brined, and washed with a bacterial culture before being transferred to the caves at Monsted where it remains for about a month.

Cave cheese has a supple texture with occasional small holes. At eight weeks it is starting to develop a fudgy aroma with a touch of meatiness, similar to Port Salut or Saint Paulin. At this stage the flavor is mild but aromatic. However, as the cheese matures to 12 or 14 weeks it takes on a much more piquant and interesting flavor.

milk	Cow's milk
style	Semihard, pressed
fat content	45 %
maturity	8 to 14 weeks
pungency	Medium
wine	Rioja

Chabichou du Poitou

Central France

*N*amed for the diminutive word for goat in the Poitevin dialect of the upper Loire Valley, this little drum-shaped cheese is best bought during the summer and early fall. The PDO version is handmade from unpasteurized milk on the farms of Poitou, but it is rare even in France.

However, the creamery-made pasteurized versions are good and widely available. They will be labeled Chabichou without the "du Poitou" and with the designation "*Laitier*." Others are known as Cabrichou, Chabi, or Cabrichiu.

All versions have a natural beige rind which occasionally develops a little blue mottling as it ripens. The white paste is firm and chewy when the cheese it is young, but ripens to a moist, almost spreadable, texture. The taste moves from mild and sweet to

milk	Goat's milk
style	Firm to soft, natural rind
fat content	45 %
maturity	2 to 3 weeks
pungency	Mild to medium
wine	Sauvignon Blanc when young and Cabernet Franc when older

a much more nutty and piquant flavor when it is older. All cheeses have quite a "goaty" aroma.

Serve Chabichou with crusty white rolls or add to a cheese board with a selection of other goat's milk cheeses. Slice the young cheese into salads and dress with toasted pine nuts, lemon juice, and olive oil. Use more mature cheeses to give an interesting flavor to savory flans or to sauces for vegetables such as cauliflower and broccoli.

VARIATIONS

Cabecou: Strictly speaking this is not a variation at all but another cheese in its own right from the Languedoc region of southwest France. It merely shares the same diminutive name for goat, this time in the Languedoc dialect. Cabecou is made in very small discs of various sizes and varies from very white, soft, and mild to bluish, hard, and strong. The best version of this cheese is Cabecou d'En-traygues from Aquitaine. Serve smallest versions on toothpicks at a cocktail buffet and larger ones with salad leaves and sliced oranges.

Chabis Sussex Goat Cheese: This small cylinder-shaped cheese with a flattened base is made by Kevin and Alison Blunt in East Sussex. Unpasteurized milk is used and gives a very creamy texture which melts in the mouth. The flavor is sweet with a goaty tang.

Tomato Chabichou

Spoon the seeds and centers out of 12 tomato halves and arrange on a bed of salad leaves. Chop a small bunch of watercress and mix with 4 chopped scallions, 12 seeded and chopped grapes, and 1 or 2 small goat cheeses, chopped into small pieces. Bind all the ingredients together with a little plain yogurt and spoon into the prepared tomato halves.

RECIPE

Chaource

Northeast France

This soft cheese from the Champagne region is named for its home town. It is richly delicious at all stages of its development, and goes very well with the famous wine from the same region.

Chaource comes in 1 lb 2 oz or 9 oz flat drum shapes with an edible white rind which may be mottled with red patches. The PDO cheeses are made in small dairies from unpasteurized milk. Other cheeses are factory made from pasteurized milk.

In the young cheese the paste is light yellow in color with a chalky texture. As it ripens it becomes very runny around the edges and through to the center. The flavor of the young cheese is rich and mild, maturing to rich and nutty.

Serve spread on toast or muffins, or present as the dessert course with fresh summer fruits. Try it melted over baked potatoes.

milk	Unpasteurized cow's milk
style	Soft bloomy rind
fat content	50 %
maturity	2 to 8 weeks
pungency	Mild
wine	Champagne or a good red Burgundy

Cheddar

Southwest England

$\mathcal{C}$heddar is the most widely made cheese in the world and as a result it is often known by the derogatory title of "mousetrap cheese." In fact top-quality Cheddar, both farmhouse and factory made, is very good indeed but much of the mass-produced cheese is bland and rubbery, bordering on tasteless.

A small amount of real farmhouse cheese is still made in the Cheddar area and in other parts of the southwest of England. The cheese is traditionally drum-shaped, weighs up to 61 lb, and is bound with a bandage to ensure a good hard grayish-brown rind. Cheeses may be matured for anything from six to 18 months

Cheddar has a smooth and fairly hard texture which should neither bend nor crumble. The paste is golden yellow in color, darkening a little with age. The flavor starts off fairly mild and meadowsweet with nutty tones, often with a light salty tang. It matures to a strong, full, wonderfully nutty taste with a real piquancy to it. Older cheeses attack the tongue with their salty acidity.

right: *Eggplant and Tomato Gratin.*

milk	Cow's milk
style	Hard, pressed, cloth-covered rind
fat content	45 to 48 %
maturity	3 months to 3 years
pungency	Mild to strong
wine	Chianti or Californian Zinfandel

After a year or so these cheeses may develop small crystals which are crunchy on the palate. These are not salt crystals, as is sometimes supposed, but casein crystals. This is a perfectly natural phenomenon. The crystals can be quite pronounced in cheeses which have been matured for two or three years such as those from New Zealand.

A good farmhouse Cheddar deserves to have the cheese course to itself. Simply serve with good crackers and celery stalks. Of course, farmhouse Cheddar is also the base for the original plowman's platter but do not spoil it all by serving cheap vinegar-soaked pickles. Look for good-quality pickles or make your own.

Cheddar melts easily and is one of the traditional choices for cooking. A small amount of a well-matured cheese gives an excellent flavor to any dish without smothering it. It is usually best to shred the cheese before adding to the other ingredients.

Good Cheddar cheese will keep its flavor for at least two weeks if it is well wrapped and kept in the refrigerator. Wrap in plastic wrap or put into a plastic box. If any mold starts to grow on the cheese, simply scrape it off.

On the farm, Cheddar may be made from unpasteurized or pasteurized whole milk. A starter culture and then rennet is used to set the curd. Once this has happened the curd is

left: *Top Paddock Cheddar.*

cut into pea-size pieces and heated very gently. As the whey is drawn off, the curds form one cohesive mass. This is then cut into thick blocks the size of cinder blocks. These are stacked on top of one another and turned so that the rest of the whey drains off. This is the cheddaring process which gives the cheese its special texture. Finally the curd is milled again, salted, packed into molds, and pressed. Traditional producers bandage the cheeses prior to storage. Others shape the cheese into large blocks which are then wrapped in plastic.

If the cheesemaker really knows his or her job, the taste and flavor of the plastic-wrapped cheese will be different than that of traditionally bound cheese, but just as good in its own way. Factory-made cheese is nearly always produced in blocks. Some of it is excellent, but sadly most of it is not.

In addition to regular Cheddar, some factories now produce a large amount of cheese flavored with a variety of ingredients such as cumin, peppercorns, beer, garlic, parsley, nuts, raisins, and sweet pickle. Red Windsor, for example, is mixed with elderberry wine. Some cheeses are smoked or layered with other cheese.

Lye Cross Cheese Straws

Eat these scrumptious cheese straws within a day or two—if they last that long! Sift a scant 1 cup whole-wheat flour into a bowl with a teaspoon of mustard powder and some salt. Blend 6 Tbsp butter and add 1 cup shredded Lye Cross Cheddar. Mix to a pastrylike consistency with a beaten egg and a little milk. Roll the mixture out and cut into fingers. Lay the fingers out evenly on a baking tray and bake in the oven for about 10 minutes at 375°F. Serve hot or cold, on their own or with a sauce for dipping.

RECIPE

English Farmhouse Cheddar: There are only a very few farms making Cheddar from unpasteurized milk. In Somerset they include Keen's Mature Cheddar with its fresh cobnut aroma and strong, but not overpowering, salty tang and nutty flavor. The year- to 18-month-old cheese may develop a few casein crystals and even a blue vein. Even more complex is prize-winning Montgomery Cheddar from Manor Farm near Yeovil. This cheese has a really spicy aroma and a wonderfully complex flavor. Lye Cross Organic Cheddar is also made in Somerset but from organic milk which is pasteurized. The cheese is matured for a year and has a good tangy aroma. It is well flavored with a rich nuttiness and an overall lemony bite to it. Quicke's of Devon is a much larger-scale operation where cheeses are made from both pasteurized and unpasteurized milk. Many traditional techniques have been retained but the cheeses do not always have the flavor of Keen's and Montgomery's Cheddars.

Cheddar-style Cheeses: Some very good cheeses made to Cheddar recipes come from outside the traditional Cheddar region. They are distinct from the West Country Cheddars but they are excellent. Lincolnshire Poacher is one of these. It is made from unpasteurized milk and is quite hard in texture with a full-bodied and complex aroma and flavor, and with an almost bittersweet taste. Another example is Tyn Grub from South Wales. This cheese is more herbaceous and acidic than most Cheddars.

Scottish Farmhouse Cheddar: Jeff Reade, on the Isle of Mull, makes an excellent handmade Cheddar-type cheese from unpasteurized milk from his own herd and matures it at the Tobermory distillery. It is very dense in texture and has a powerful spicy bite.

Dunlop: Dunlop is a factory-made cheese very similar to block Cheddar except that it is usually paler in color, and lighter and moister in texture. It lacks the bite that most Cheddar has. An exception is that made by Ann Dorward in Ayrshire.

Arran and Orkney: These are Dunlop-style cheeses made on the Isle of Arran and in the Orkneys respectively. There is one producer of traditional Orkney cheese which is more like the Dales cheeses (see page 112) although perhaps a little harder and even sharper.

American Cheddar Cheese: Nearly all the Cheddar cheese sold in the United States is factory produced. It is often known simply as "American." It comes in all shapes and sizes and much of it is heavily dyed to a deep orange color and often waxed black, red, or orange. Coon is a factory-made Cheddar hybrid which is largely confined to the Midwest. Tillamook is one of the few factory-produced Cheddars in America which has a real taste and flavor. It is made in large quantities at the Tillamook Cheese Company in Oregon. There are both annatto colored and undyed cheeses as well as a range of cheeses of different ages. Vintage Tillamook is matured for 18 months. However, there are a few smaller producers who are making good Cheddar cheese, some from raw milk. They include the Loleta Cheese Factory and the Vella Cheese Company in California and the Rogue River Valley Creamery in Oregon. Three more creameries which produce first-class Cheddar are all situated in Vermont. They are the Cabot Creamery—look out for the two-year-old Private Broth Cheddar, the Grafton Village Company—another excellent two-year old Cheddar here, and the prize-winning Shelburne Farms.

Canadian Cheddar Cheese: Though mainly factory produced, Canadian Cheddar is uniformly good. Black Diamond Cheddar is the best-known brand outside of Canada.

Australian Cheddar Cheese: Like the Cheddar of North America most Australian Cheddar is factory made and not usually all that interesting. Coon is simply an Australian brand of Cheddar and Cheedam is a kind of cross between a Cheddar and an Edam cheese. Top Paddock is a small producer in Bena, Victoria. They produce a small Cheddar which is matured for nine months to develop a much fuller and more interesting flavor.

New Zealand Cheddar Cheese: Like Canada, New Zealand produces Cheddar of excellent quality in large factories. New Zealanders like their Cheddar relatively young but the Anchor Food company ships quantities of their best cheese to the UK where it is matured for another year or two, resulting in cheese which is two or even three years of age. These cheeses have a wonderfully full and fruity flavor with touches of caramel and spice.

Cheshire

Northwest England

*T*his could be England's oldest cheese. It was mentioned in the Domesday Book and its origins go back to Roman times. As well as being made in Cheshire, it is also made in parts of Shropshire and Staffordshire in farmhouses (rare) and large creameries. Factory-made Cheshire often comes in block form and, as is so often the case, there is a substantial difference in quality between the farmhouse and the factory cheese.

Farmhouse Cheshire is produced in 40 lb cylinders which may be waxed or may be cloth bandaged like Cheddar. Look out for cheeses from Overton Hall, Mollington Grange Farm, and from Mrs. Appleby at Abbey Farm. The latter makes the only unpasteurized clothbound Cheshire cheese available today.

Cheshire cheese has a loose and crumbly texture, much more friable and moist than many other hard cheeses. White Cheshire is

milk	Cow's milk
style	Hard, pressed, cloth bandaged or wrapped in cheesecloth and waxed
fat content	45 to 48 %
maturity	4 to 8 weeks
pungency	Mild but lightly tangy
wine	Mersault or New World Cabernet Sauvignon

pale in color while Red Cheshire is a deep peachy orange color which comes from annatto dye. Both types have a mild and lightly salty taste which is attributed to the salty soil of the Cheshire plain. Mature cheeses acquire more piquancy with age.

Serve at any time of the day as a snack with fruit or crudités, on a cheese board, or with sweet pickles, radishes, and celery on a plowman's platter. Cheshire cheese was traditionally served with farmhouse fruitcake. Use in cooked dishes which require a gentle cheese flavor. Cheshire cheese seems to have a particular affinity to eggs so add to fluffy soufflé omelets.

Unlike Cheddar, Cheshire cheese does not store very well so only buy enough for your immediate requirements. Avoid dry and cracked cheese or cheese which is sweating excessively.

VARIATIONS

Blue Cheshire: Cheshire cheese turns blue very easily, and the blue versions used to be known as Green Fade. They were very rich in appearance and flavor. Blue Cheshire unfortunately ceased production in 1997 and as yet no other producer has come forward.

Gospel Green: This is a full-flavored open-textured cheese rather similar to Cheshire made by James and Cathy Lane in Surrey. It has a grassy aroma and full flavor.

Welsh Rarebit

Cheshire cheese was the original cheese used to make Welsh rarebit. Place 2 Tbsp butter in a saucepan with ¼ cup flour and 1 cup half and half beer and milk. Bring to a boil, whisking all the time with a wire whisk, until thickened. Cook for 2 minutes more and stir in 1 cup shredded Cheshire cheese, 1 tsp English mustard, and a little cayenne pepper. Pour over 4 slices of toast and brown under the broiler.

RECIPE

Chèvre

France

*C*hèvre is the generic term for French goat cheese. It comes in all shapes and sizes, some of which are listed under their own names in this cheese directory, but in many markets Chèvre is symbolized by the Chèvre Log. These are mass produced in France. They have a diameter of about two to three inches and a thin white rind. They are packed rolled in straw or plastic matting.

The paste is very white indeed and has a soft, very slightly granular texture which spreads easily. The flavor is usually very mild and lightly salty, although some have a stronger more musty flavor.

Serve in slices with crusty bread or on a bagel, and lightly broil. Serve with salads dressed with nuts, capers, or fresh herbs, and vinaigrette, or remove the rind and melt into sauces for pasta or vegetables. Chèvre does not usually taste stronger when heated.

below: *Broiled Chèvre Bagel.*

There are literally hundreds of different goat cheeses which do not naturally fit into any specific category. Here are a few which have a particularly good flavor. Some may be specific to the country in which they are produced.

FRENCH SOFT GOAT CHEESES

Charollais: Burgundian cheese made in small cylinders and sold in various states from fresh to aged. Find it in local markets in France.

Mothe-Saint-Heray: This is a good factory-made cheese which is ripened for two weeks between layers of vine or plane tree leaves.

Selles-sur-Cher: This small disc-shaped cheese comes from the Loire Valley. It is distinctive for its coating of ash which contrasts with the very white soft paste. It is soft and moist with a sweetly musty flavor. The paste becomes firmer as it matures and the flavor strengthens. See also page 202.

BRITISH SOFT GOAT CHEESES

Gedi: Mild creamy cheeses, plain or coated in herbs, made by Nachy and Betty Elkin in Hertfordshire.

Innes: Fresh farmhouse cheeses made from unpasteurized milk at Highfields Dairy in Staffordshire.

Mine-Gabhar: A soft, natural mold, ripened cheese from Luc and Anne van Kempen in County Wexford, Ireland.

Perroche: A very mild and fresh cheese from Kent. Its light lemony flavor goes well with the tarragon in which it is rolled. Also available with other herbs.

Tymsboro': A truncated pyramid made from unpasteurized milk and sprinkled with ash. The paste softens round the edges, remaining chalky in the center. It has sweetly musty flavor.

Vulscombe: Fresh unrenneted cheese made from unpasteurized milk, lighted pressed.

Wigmore: A delicate cheese made from unpasteurized milk by Anne Wigmore at Spencers Wood in Berkshire. Matured in eight weeks, it develops a distinctive "crumpled" gray crust. The paste has a supple texture and fresh, creamy flavor.

AMERICAN SOFT GOAT CHEESES

Coach Farm: This company in New York State produces an excellent range of fresh and soft cheeses in all shapes and sizes. The young cheeses are moist and flaky, and some of them are coated with herbs or spices like cumin or peppercorns.

Cypress Grove: This farm in northern California produces fresh and aged cheeses. The older cheeses have really interesting nutty, spicy flavors.

Fromagerie Belle Chèvre: Prize-winning cheeses are made by this company in Alabama. Look out for the fresh Chèvre Logs and Chèvre de Provence.

AUSTRALIAN SOFT GOAT CHEESES

Look out for cheeses from Gabrielle Kervella at Fromage Fermier in Gidegannup in Western Australia. Gabrielle traveled to France to learn the art of making Chèvre, and now she has her own herd of dairy goats.

above: *Mine-Gabhar.*

milk	Goat's milk
style	Soft, white bloomy rind
fat content	45 %
maturity	Not applicable
pungency	Mild
wine	Sauvignon Blanc wines

Colby

Wisconsin, US

𝒥nvented in the late nineteenth-century, this factory-made cheese is now a firm favorite in the United States. It is similar in flavor to everyday Cheddar but has a softer and more open, sometimes almost lacy, texture. Like most American Cheddar it is often dyed a deep orange-yellow color. The flavor is light and mild.

Crowley cheese made by the Crowley Cheese Company in Vermont is perhaps the very best flavored Colby. Young (two months) or mature (up to a year). Colby can be used instead of Cheddar for a lighter flavor and is usually used in sandwiches.

VARIATION

Longhorn: This is the name given to whole Colbys made in an elongated conical shape.

milk	Cow's milk
style	Hard, pressed
fat content	45 %
maturity	2 months
pungency	Very mild
wine	Californian Zinfandel

Comté

*T*his ancient French cheese, also known as Gruyère de Comté, is made in the region which lies between the Vosges and the Haute-Savoie. It is all made in small dairies using unpasteurized milk. Special companies (*affiners*) look after the maturing cheeses for a year or more.

Produced in large 88 lb cylinders, the cheese has a thin beige rind which thickens and hardens as the cheese matures. The dark straw-colored paste may contain some medium-size holes and has a tendency to crack on cutting.

This cheese has a wonderful floral aroma with nutty fudge flavors developing in the more mature cheese. The taste is full of nuts and toffee with a lovely long and salty finish. Older cheeses take on a strong, farmyardlike character. Serve after dinner with fruit or use in sandwiches with cold ham or French salami.

milk	Unpasteurized cow's milk
style	Hard, cooked and pressed, natural brushed rind
fat content	45 %
maturity	5 to 12 months
pungency	Medium strong
wine	Chianti Classico Riserva or Rioja

Cornish Yarg

Cornwall, England

This attractive little Cornish cheese has a unique covering of local nettle leaves which gives it a slightly vegetal or herby taste. Using nettles in this way was once quite common in this part of the world but the practice largely died out in the last century.

The name Yarg does not relate to old Cornish but is simply "gray" spelt backwards. Gray was the name of the cheese-maker who developed the cheese from some old recipes found in an attic.

The nettles give the cheese a grayish-green rind which contrasts with the very white paste. The texture is similar to Caerphilly but the flavor is not really the same. The young cheese is fresh and lemony with a touch of herbs. Older cheeses start to lose their lemony tang and develop more aromatic, peppery, and vegetal tones.

Serve with crackers and your best wines. Crumble into beet and apple salads or sprinkle over baked zucchini.

milk	Cow's milk
style	Hard, pressed, mold ripened, nettle-wrapped rind
fat content	57 %
maturity	6 to 8 weeks
pungency	Mild
wine	Good Claret or red Burgundy

Coulommiers

*T*his Brielike cheese is mainly factory made in the Ile de France near Paris. There is no standard recipe for Coulommiers and so it has never had appellation controlled (now PDO) status.

The cheese has a white, bloomy, often uneven rind with a little brown mottling as it ages. It has a faint aroma of mushrooms and the flavor is quite mild and delicate in the young cheese, becoming more pronounced as it matures. Serve on its own with grapes or use as for Brie.

VARIATION

Sharpham: This prize-winning cheese is made by Debbie Mumford from unpasteurized Jersey cow's milk at Totnes in Devon. Available in various sizes, it is ripened on the farm for five weeks before selling on.

milk	Cow's milk
style	Soft, bloomy rind
fat content	45 %
maturity	1 month
pungency	Mild
wine	Medium-bodied Côtes du Rhône

Cream Cheese

Universal

$\mathcal{T}$his is the general term which covers fresh soft cheese made with light or heavy cream. It may be farm or factory made. The cheese has a soft buttery texture and is spreadable. It has a rich, full, often buttery flavor, sometimes with a mild tang to it.

Cream cheese can be served on its own, on open sandwiches, on canapés, or with salads. Use in cooking to enrich sauces, soups, mousses, and stuffings. It is also the essential ingredient in any cheesecake, be it sweet or savory, and as such can be baked or simply set in the refrigerator.

Savory Cheesecake

Line an 8-inch cake pan with pastry. Heat 1 tbsp butter, add 1 large onion, sliced and cook until soft. Beat 4 eggs. Mix 8 oz cream cheese and 8 oz curd cheese with the onions, chopped chives, pepper, and salt. Fold this mixture into the eggs and spoon into the cake pan. Bake at 350°F for 40 minutes.

VARIATIONS

Mascarpone: This Italian specialty is not really a cheese as no starter or rennet is used in its manufacture. Instead the cream is mixed with lemon juice or citric acid and hung in cheesecloth to encourage the water to drain away. It used to be freshly made in the food store and sold directly from the cheesecloth draining bags. Today it is more likely to be made in a factory-based centrifuge and packed into sealed cartons. Mascarpone has a smooth and creamy taste and texture. There should not be any lumps in the spoonable paste. It goes with most foods whether they are sweet or savory. In Italy is it used in much the same way as heavy cream is used elsewhere. Mascarpone is an essential ingredient in the popular Italian dessert, Tiramisu, which is made with ladyfingers soaked in coffee, and layered with egg yolks, cocoa, and Strega liqueur.

Caboc: A heavy cream cheese coated in oatmeal and made in Scotland.

Neufchâtel: A marketing name given to cream cheese in northwest and midwest America. It bears no relation to the rare French PDO cheese of that name from Normandy.

Philadelphia: An American brand of pasteurized cream cheese now marketed worldwide.

milk	Cow's cream
style	Soft, fresh
fat content	Cream cheese 45% plus, heavy cream cheese 65 % plus
maturity	Fresh
pungency	Mild
wine	Pinot Noir

Crottin de Chavignol

Central France

$\mathcal{G}$oats grazing around the vineyards of Sancerre in the Loire Valley supply the milk for Crottin de Chavignol. Protected by the French appellation controllée (now PDO) system, the genuine cheese is made only in the village of Chavignol. However, there are some very good Crottin de Chèvre made in the surrounding villages.

Produced in small 2 oz drums, the cheese has a white rind which darkens with maturity through blue-gray to black. The paste is very white and firm, creamy to start with and hardening as it matures. The flavor is lightly flinty with nuts, turning spicier as it ages.

Serve as part of a cheese course or on its own with crusty whole-wheat bread. Cut in half and broil on rounds of toast for appetizers or salads, or bake whole and serve with a good dressing.

milk	Goat's milk
style	Soft to firm, natural rind
fat content	45 %
maturity	2 to 3 months
pungency	Mild to medium
wine	Red or white Sancerre

The word "crottin" refers to the dark color of the mature cheese and this is the way the locals traditionally ate it.

Curd or Cottage Cheese

Universal

$\mathcal{T}$hese terms used to mean traditional curd cheeses made on the farm by souring fresh milk or by renneting pasteurized milk and draining the curds. But today they also mean factory-produced products like Fromage Frais, Quark, and American-style crumbly cottage cheese.

These cheeses are extremely versatile. Serve with any kind of bread, with salads, on crispbread, with fruit, particularly apples or pears, or mix into dips (see below) or spreads with chopped fresh herbs and other flavorings.

Though some of the products are very creamy, they all behave like cheese on cooking. This means that they will blend well to create creamy sauces and soups but if heated beyond a certain level they will seize up as the milk proteins separate from the fat. Use to make stuffings and fillings, in curd tarts and cheesecakes, or substitute for higher-fat cream cheeses if you prefer.

left: *Cod's Roe Dip.*

VARIATIONS

Farmer's curd cheese: This is usually curdless and may be grainy or creamy, depending on the fat content. It is very much a local product which is sold from the farmhouse. Scottish Crowdie is an example of a simple, fresh farmhouse cheese curdled with rennet. It is low in fat and crumbly, but more moist than cottage cheese. It has a good lemony tang to it. Some versions are flavored, such as Hramsa with cream and wild garlic, and Gruth Dhu with cream, and then it is rolled in peppercorns and oatmeal. In the United States, Sweet Home Farms in Alabama and Cabot Creamery in Vermont both make farmhouse-type cottage cheese.

Fromage Frais: This is the generic name given to a range of types and brands of French fresh soft cheese. Fromage frais is mostly factory made with a starter culture alone or with a starter culture and rennet. The fat content varies from 0 to 60 %. It is very soft, creamy, and mild in flavor.

Paneer: This is a very simple form of pressed curd cheese, which was traditionally made in the home in India and used in vegetarian curry dishes. It is now being made by dairies in other parts of the world. It has a relatively firm texture and a very bland taste that takes up other flavors well.

Quark: This is simply the German name for curds and it is Germany's most popular cheese. In effect, Quark is the German equivalent of Fromage Frais. It is factory produced using a variety of methods, including the centrifugal system that separates the curds and whey. Like Fromage Frais the fat content varies from 0 to 60% but they are all smooth and thick, with a texture somewhere between that of yogurt and cream cheese. Quark is white in color and has a clean, mild flavor, sometimes with just a hint of acidity.

Demi-Sel and Petit Suisse: These are firmer, fattier types of curd cheese.

Vulscombe: This is an English unrenneted, lightly pressed, goat's milk cheese from Devon

American-style cottage cheese: This is spoonable and has moist granules of curd. It is usually made from skim milk and is high in calcium and low in fat. All cottage cheese is pretty mild in flavor.

Dales Cheeses

Northern England

*T*here has been a great revival of farmhouse cheeses based on old recipes from the Dales of the north Pennines in the north of England, the example above being Cotherstone.

VARIATIONS

Cotherstone: This once famous cheese is again being made in Teesdale from unpasteurized milk. Joan Cross produces a crumbly cheese which is also soft and moist. The cheese is usually eaten after two to three weeks and has a refreshingly sour but buttery flavor. Some cheesemongers like to mature the cheese for longer to achieve a firmer paste and stronger flavor.

Coverdale: This cheese has been revived after an absence of fifty years by Fountains Dairy Products in Ripon. It is a tall, cylindrical, cloth-wrapped cheese. The cheese is matured for a month to give a typically soft and crumbly Dales cheese with a mildly acidic flavor. Some cheeses are flavored with chives.

Ribblesdale: This is another cheese made in the old Dales style with a moist and open-textured paste which melts in the mouth. It has a creamy flavor. It may also be smoked or flavored with garlic.

Swaledale: This is a cheese similar to Wensleydale but softer and perhaps more lemony in flavor. It is made by David Reed in Richmond. Oak-smoked versions, and cheeses flavored with herbs and beer, are also available.

Danish Blue

Denmark

*A*lso known as Danblu, the Danes invented this blue cheese in 1927 as an alternative to Roquefort. Though quite unlike Roquefort, the cheese has been a huge commercial success and is sold worldwide.

Danish Blue is factory made from pasteurized milk which has been homogenized to ensure a smooth curd and clear taste. It is rindless and comes in foil-wrapped shapes. The paste is milk white with very blue veins and a few irregularly distributed holes. It is soft and a little crumbly but surprisingly easy to slice. The flavor is distinctively sharp and salty.

Serve on open sandwiches or in club sandwiches with ham, lettuce, and tomato. Mix with butter to make a piquant spread or crumble into salad dressings. Danish Blue can be used in cooking, but it needs to be used sparingly and extra salt may not be needed. Try it in quiches, soups, and sauces for broccoli or cabbage.

right: *Mix Danish Blue with Ricotta and Fromage Frais to make a salad dressing.*

milk	Homogenized cow's milk
style	Semihard, blue veined, pressed
fat content	50 to 60 %
maturity	7 to 8 weeks
pungency	Strong and salty
wine	Schnapps

VARIATIONS

Layered Blue: Danish Blue is sometimes layered with cream cheese and shaped into a loaf. This looks attractive on a cheese board and serves to soften the salty attack of the cheese.

Jutland and Mellow Blue: These have a higher fat content than regular Danish Blue and are rather milder in flavor.

Saint Agur: This is an octagonal, French factory-made cheese which resembles Danish Blue, although the flavor is milder and less salty.

Blue: This is the general term used for American factory-made blue cheese. It resembles Danish Blue with its tasty, although rather one-dimensional flavor.

RECIPE

Savory Truffles

Crush 4 oz water biscuits and mix with the same amount of each of the following: soft cheese, shredded Edam, and crumbled Danish Blue. Add 2 oz each chopped dates and walnuts, and a little shredded orange rind. If the mixture is too stiff, add a little mayonnaise. Shape the mixture into small balls and coat in toasted sesame seeds, poppy seeds, or chopped fresh herbs. Serve with toothpicks.

Edam

The Netherlands

*D*espite having a long history, real farmhouse Edam has disappeared and with it its original sharp identity. Today Edam is a pleasant but rather bland factory-produced cheese.

Edam is known for its distinctive red wax coating, but this only appears on cheeses for export. Those destined for the home market are sold with their natural thin yellow rind exposed. The buttercup yellow paste is firm but springy, although not usually as rubbery as young factory-made Gouda. Edam has a lightly spicy aroma and easy taste with a slightly salty flavor lingering on the palate.

Edam is made from partially skimmed, pasteurized milk and so it has a relatively low fat content. In The Netherlands, Edam is served in thin slices cut with a special handheld cheese slicer and is traditionally served for breakfast, but it is also popular as a snack on its own or in salads.

milk	Partially skimmed cow's milk
style	Hard, pressed, natural rind
fat content	40 %
maturity	6 to 8 weeks
pungency	Mild
wine	Full-bodied Syrah or Shiraz

Emmental

Central Switzerland

Commonly known quite simply as "Swiss" cheese, Emmental has many imitators. The original cheese came from the soft meadows of the Emme river valley near Bern. The farmers here have been making the cheese since 1293. At that time cheese was made on the Alps where the cattle spent the summer but today it is also made in the neighboring lowlands.

Emmental is one of the largest cheeses in the world. Each flat-sided, wheel-shaped cheese is made by hand from unpasteurized milk. More than 264 gallons of milk is required for one cheese. It has a characteristic smooth pale yellow rind. The flexible paste is a lovely deep yellow color with holes the size of cherries, walnuts, or even golf balls. A really good Emmental has a wonderfully complex aroma of meadows and flowers with raisins and wood fires. The flavor, too, is strong and fruity with a mature woody finish.

milk	Unpasteurized cow's milk
style	Semihard, cooked, and pressed, brushed and oiled natural rind
fat content	45 %
maturity	4 to 12 months
pungency	Mild to medium
wine	Full-bodied Syrah or Shiraz

Emmental is delicious served on its own, so do as the Swiss do and serve it thinly sliced with a handheld cheese slicer at breakfast or as part of a selection of cheeses at lunch or supper time. It is also very good diced into salads with chopped mushrooms, cornichons, bell peppers, and scallions. Emmental is also very good melted on bagels or toast or in *croque monsieur*. Mature Emmental melts better and has a better flavor in cooked dishes than the young cheese, but the end result will still be fairly stringy. Use in gratin dishes, sauces, and fondue.

Emmental cheese is made by mixing the morning milk with that from the previous evening. A starter culture which includes the hole inducing (proprionic) bacteria and rennet is added to the milk which coagulates within a half hour.

The curds are cut in a crisscross fashion with a special instrument made of tightly strung wires, aptly called a cheese harp. They are then heated and continually cut and stirred until the cheese grains become harder and drier. They are then removed from the vat in a large cheesecloth bag and transferred to a cheese press. The following day the cheese is dipped into a salt solution and left to dry out for ten to 14 days, after which it is moved to warmer fermentation cellars where the holes start to form in the curd.

above: *Swiss Cheese Bagel.*

The final ripening takes place in cool cellars. During the whole of the ripening process the cheeses have to be turned regularly. In the past this had to be done by hand and the strong muscles of the cheesemakers were much feared in the wrestling ring. Today machinery does the job.

By law, no Swiss Emmental cheese may be exported until it has reached four months old, at which age it is still regarded as a young cheese. The rind of these cheeses is always stamped with the word "Switzerland."

French Emmental: The French Comté region of France near the Swiss border has been making Emmental cheese almost as long as have the Swiss. Indeed, the locals would have you believe that they got in first! The recipe for French Emmental is just the same as for Swiss Emmental but the cheese tends to be more bulbous than the flat-sided Swiss cheeses. French Emmental is all factory made but the flavor is very good indeed. You may have to pay more for it than for the Swiss version because demand in the home market is such that the French do not really need to export.

Allgau Emmenthaler: This is the German version of Emmental. It is made in the Allgau region of Bavaria from pasteurized milk. It is usually sold at a younger age than other styles of Emmental and so does not have as much flavor.

Austrian Emmenthaler: Another factory-made cheese, often called Austrian Swiss; it has a tendency to be rather rubbery and tasteless.

American and Australian Swiss: Locally produced imitations of Swiss Emmental, such as the American Swiss Lace, which are popular in their own countries.

Jarlsberg: Strictly speaking this is not an Emmental cheese but it is similar and it is used in much the same way, particularly in the United States. It is based on an old Norwegian recipe which was revived in the 1950s. It usually has a softer texture than Emmental but can be very rubbery. There are very large holes in the pale paste. The aroma is reminiscent of sour milk with nuts and the taste is oddly dry and nutty sometimes with sour raisins. It does not have the fruitiness or savory bite of a good Emmental.

Svenbo: This is a very mild version of Emmental from Denmark. It has a dry yellow rind and pale yellow paste with large round holes. It has a lightly nutty flavor.

above: *Jarlsberg.*

English Hard Goat Cheese

England

$\mathcal{T}$he start of the 1980s saw a blossoming of English farm-house cheeses which continues today. Many of these cheeses are made from goat's milk. Here are three of the leading contenders, Ticklemore being the one featured above.

VARIATIONS

Mendip: Mary Holbrook at Sleight Farm at Timsbury in the West Country makes this firm cheese from unpasteurized milk. It is formed in a 3 lb plastic basket mold which leaves a distinct impression on the oiled rind. The cheese may be matured from two through eight months. The young cheese has a pale yellow creamy paste with small holes. It has a lightly acidic tang and fresh fruity taste.

Ticklemore: This hard cheese is made by hand from unpasteurized milk at Totnes in Devon. It is pressed in 5 lb spheres in basket molds and matured for two and a half months. It has a hard dry natural rind and white to cream-colored paste, which becomes darker near the rind. Small holes are scattered through the slightly crumbly paste. The cheese has an aroma of cooked mushrooms and tastes nutty with a touch of caramel and good acidic finish. It is particularly delicious with whole-wheat bread.

Cerney Village: This is made in Gloucestershire from pasteurized goat's milk. It is a matured firm cheese with a herbaceous yet "goaty" flavor to it.

Epoisse

Northwest France

*T*his small Burgundian cheese was the favorite cheese of Porthos in *The Three Musketeers* and it is a candidate for the top ten most pungent French cheeses. It is sometimes macerated in burgundy *marc* to become an even stronger Fromage Fort. The PDO cheeses are made from unpasteurized milk and are not available in the United States.

Produced in small 1 lb discs, the cheese has a pale brick-colored rind which is washed in the local *eau de vie* as it ripens. The paste is soft and supple. The cheese has a very strong farmyardlike flavor with a whiff of burnt tires and ammonia which comes from the rind. The paste smells much softer although still with a sharp tangy aroma. The flavor is deliciously rustic but also creamy and refreshing with sour lemons lingering on the palate.

milk	Cow's milk
style	Soft, washed rind
fat content	45 %
maturity	6 to 8 weeks
pungency	Pungent
wine	Mature red Burgundy

above: *An adventurous French tasting board (see page 44).*

Because of the strong flavor of this cheese, it is best served on its own, rather than used in cooking. Serve it as part of a cheese board—you might wish to include it with a selection of other French cheeses, such as Bleu d'Auvergne, Valency, Explotateur, Tomme de Savoie, and Banon. To get the most out of the unique flavor of this cheese, serve it simply with plain unsalted crackers such as water biscuits or a fresh baguette.

When buying this cheese, make sure it fills its box and has not shrunk away from the outside edges, as this indicates that it is past its best. Once cut, Epoisse should be eaten immediately as it does not store well, even in the refrigerator and is likely to cause unwanted odors that may flavor other food it is stored next to.

above: *A fresh Epoisse should fill the box in which it is sold.*

Esrom

Denmark

*I*nvented in the 1930s, this cheese was said to resemble Port Salut and was, for a time, named Danish Port Salut. In fact, it is a much more interesting cheese than Port Salut. In the 1950s it was renamed for a long-forgotten cheese made by the monks of Esrom.

Esrom is made in flat rectangular shapes and is usually wrapped in foil. The yellow paste has a supple texture with irregularly shaped holes. The flavor is quite rich and aromatic and seems to grow on the palate. It gains even more spicy flavors as it ages and so often tastes better when it has been exported because it is more mature.

Serve as part of a cheese course or cheese buffet. Slice and serve, as the Danes do, for breakfast or use on open sandwiches with orange segments and sliced raw onion, or melt over hamburgers. Well wrapped and kept in a cool place, Esrom will keep for a couple of weeks.

milk	Cow's milk
style	Semihard, washed rind
fat content	45 to 60 %
maturity	10 to 12 weeks
pungency	Medium
wine	Valpolicella

Explorateur

Central France

*T*his aristocrat of triple-cream cheeses was invented in 1958 at the time the rocket Explorer was in the news. The French dairy which invented the cheese decided on a topical name and a picture of the rocket still appears on the wrapping.

Explorateur was one of the first cheeses to be created after the triple-cream classification was defined as a cheese with a butterfat content of 75 percent or more. This is achieved by adding a great deal of cream to the milk before coagulation.

The cheese is produced in small 9$^{1}/_{2}$ oz discs with a light, downy white rind. The deep ivory paste is very soft and creamy. The flavor is very rich and mild, deepening a little with maturity.

Serve with a platter of fresh fruit at the end of the meal or spread on a baguette to make an excellent snack. Use in Chicken Kiev in place of garlic butter or for a rich sauce for squab chicken.

milk	Cow's milk and cream
style	Soft, triple-cream bloomy rind
fat content	75 %
maturity	2 weeks
pungency	Mild
wine	Dry sparkling

Feta

Greece

𝓕eta is so popular in Greece that they actually import it from other producers such as Denmark. In Greece, Feta cheese was traditionally made from ewe's, or sometimes a mixture of ewe's and goat's, milk and the cheese had a definite taste as well as the salty flavor which comes from brining the fresh cheese.

Now cow's milk is also used and you can no longer be quite so sure of the flavor. In Greek shops, Feta cheese is sold in large blocks or slices known as *fetes*—hence the name. There is no rind and the paste is very white and dense but crumbles easily. There are small holes and cracks scattered throughout the paste. The cheese has a milky aroma and a creamy texture in the mouth. The taste is sharp and salty, but not unpleasantly so.

Avoid cheeses which have been in the brine for too long. They will have little flavor and be hard and difficult to crumble. Shrink-wrapped cheeses may also exhibit these defects, so try and buy your Feta from the brine bath and taste to check its texture.

In Greece Feta cheese is eaten at all times of the day. It makes a healthy breakfast with bread, a good lunch with tomatoes and olives, or an excellent snack on its own.

milk	Ewe's, goat's, and cow's
style	Hard but fresh cheese
fat content	40 to 50 %
maturity	1 to 3 weeks
pungency	Mild but salty
wine	Ouzo

Alternatively crumble over salads (see opposite), use in phyllo pastry parcels with vegetables such as spinach or mushrooms, or deep fry in bread crumbs. If it too salty for your tastes, simply soak the cheese in milk for a while before using. When storing, it is best to keep it in a plastic container with a little of the brine bath to ensure it stays in good condition.

right: *Feta is ideal for use in salads; cut into cubes and sprinkle over.*

VARIATIONS

Danish and other Feta cheeses: Most of these are made from pasteurized cow's milk and often bear no relationship to Greek Feta cheese.

English Farmhouse Feta: A number of small producers, such as Mary Holbrook at Sleight Farm near Bath, Shepherds Purse Cheesemakers in North Yorkshire, and the Sussex High Weald Dairy, are making excellent Feta from unpasteurized sheep's milk.

Timboon Gourmet Feta: This is an award-winning organic Feta from a small creamery in Victoria, Australia.

Broiled Feta Cheese with Olives

Serve with a glass of Ouzo and you will immediately be transported off to Greece. Crumble plenty of Feta cheese over pita bread which has been split open and toasted on one side. Drizzle with Greek extra virgin olive oil and place under a moderate broiler for a couple of minutes. Transfer to serving plates and top with more warm olive oil and lemon juice. Add black olives and fresh oregano, and serve.

RECIPE

Fontina

Northwest Italy

*G*enuine Fontina is made only in the steep-sided Val d'Aosta in the Italian Alps near Mont Blanc and the French border. Each cheese has its name and that of the local cooperative stenciled on the rind. In summer the cheeses are made in the chalets of the alpine pastures, and in winter in creameries lower down the valley.

Produced in various size wheels from 18 to 40 lb, Fontina has a creamy brown rind which is thin and oily. The paste is smooth and buttery, almost spreadable, when young. It has a pale straw color and a few small holes fairly evenly distributed throughout. As the cheese matures it becomes darker and much drier. The young cheese is milky and lightly scented from the alpine meadows. The older cheese develops an earthy but fruity aroma with a mellow flavor of nuts and fruit.

Serve with celery or grapes, or use in toasted sandwiches. Fontina is a marvelous cheese for cooking as it melts into a creamy mass that is good for sauces. Fonduta, the Piedmontese version of fondue, is based on Fontina with butter, eggs, and wild mushrooms.

right: *Spinach Lasagne with Fontina Cheese Sauce.*

Fontinella, Fontella, Fontal: These are all brand names used by the big creameries of the Po Valley on their lookalike Fontina cheeses. They are mildly pleasant but they are not the real thing.

Danish Fontina: This red-waxed cheese is nothing like the real thing. It is bland and rubbery.

Roth Kase Fontina: This American creamery in Monroe, Wisconsin, uses a heat-treatment technique which does not steal all the flavor from the milk and the cheese is very good.

Val d'Aosta Baked Pasta

Fry some garlic with 2 fine chopped onions. Add 2 chopped eggplant, a chopped fennel bulb, 2 Tbsp tomato paste, and ³/₄ cup broth, and bring to a boil. Simmer for about 10 minutes until the eggplant begins to soften. Cook 9 oz fusilli in boiling water for 3 to 4 minutes. Line a small baking pan with foil, leaving enough to fold over the top. Add the well-drained pasta and pour on the eggplant mixture, 4 chopped tomatoes, 2 cups shredded mature Fontina cheese, and plenty of salt and ground black pepper. Close up the foil, leaving a space above the pasta. Bake for about 15 minutes at 375°F. Serve from the foil with more Fontina cheese.

milk	Unpasteurized cow's milk
style	Semihard, cooked and pressed, brushed rind
fat content	45 %
maturity	4 months
pungency	Mild
wine	Barbaresco or Recioto della Valpolicella

RECIPE

Forme d'Ambert

Central France

*T*his ancient French cheese from the Auvergne was being made long before English Stilton, which it somewhat resembles, was even thought of. Now mainly factory produced from pasteurized milk, it still maintains its old standards.

The cheese has a deep cylindrical shape about 8 inches high and 4 to 5 inches in diameter. There is a rough gray-brown rind and firm ivory paste with liberal greenish-blue veining. It has an interesting aroma of roasted nuts and a fruity flavor. Eat with crisp apples or juicy pears, or serve with Port at the end of a meal.

VARIATION

Forme de Montbrison and Forme de Forez: These are very similar cheeses from neighboring villages.

milk	Cow's milk
style	Semihard blue, lightly pressed, natural rind
fat content	45 %
maturity	4 to 5 months
pungency	Medium to strong
wine	Côtes du Rhône

Gaperon

Central France

$\mathscr{T}$his is a really gutsy cheese from the Auvergne. Its pungent flavor comes partly from the cheese itself but also from the local garlic which is combined with it. The cheeses used to be hung from the rafters or at the kitchen window to ripen and, it was said, a farmer's wealth could be gauged by counting them.

Shaped like a flat-bottomed ball, Gaperon has a white bloomy rind which turns a deep straw color as it ripens. The cheese is bound with raffia or ribbon with a label on the top or bottom. The paste, too, ripens from chalky white to ivory when it becomes quite soft and supple. Peppercorns sometimes join garlic in the flavorings for this cheese, and the aroma and taste of the cheese is unmistakable.

Serve on its own with robust bread. Do not add it to a cheese board—the assault on the taste buds means that you will be unable to taste milder cheeses after eating it.

milk	Partially skimmed cow's milk
style	Soft, pressed with flavorings, bloomy rind
fat content	30 to 45 %
maturity	2 weeks
pungency	Very strong
wine	Vodka

Gjetost

Norway

No traditional breakfast would be complete in Norway without this sweet red cheese. It is made from the whey or buttermilk which is heated very slowly until the water has evaporated and the milk sugar forms a kind of brown caramelized paste. At this stage milk or cream may be added to change the fat content of the finished product.

Produced in squares this cheese has no rind and is sold as soon as it is made. The texture may be hard or soft but it all has an unmistakable sweet, almost fudgy, caramel taste. Serve with fruit, such as grapefruit, on rye bread or crispbread, or with rich fruitcake.

milk	Goat's and cow's milk whey
style	Cooked whey, pressed
fat content	Variable
maturity	Fresh
pungency	Sweet
wine	Madeira

VARIATION

Ekte: This is Gjetost made from goat's milk alone. It has a sharper taste than that made from mixed milks.

Gloucester

England

$\mathcal{L}$ike Cheddar, Gloucester cheese has suffered in the transition from small-scale to factory production, and the distinction between Double and Single Gloucester has become blurred. These traditional forms of the cheese are only produced on a very few farms today.

Single Gloucester was originally made from the evening's unpasteurized milk which was skimmed and then combined with whole milk from the morning milking. This was a firm but supple cheese intended for quick ripening. It was generally eaten on the farm where it was made. Today, Single Gloucester is made from the skim milk of one or both of the milkings. It is made in smaller sizes than Double Gloucester. Smart's Farmhouse Single Gloucester is aged for one to three months. It has a thin whitish-yellow rind and firm, dark ivory paste. The texture is dry and crumbly, and the cheese

milk	Cow's milk
style	Hard, cloth-wrapped or waxed rind
fat content	48 %
maturity	6 to 9 months
pungency	Single: medium. Double: strong but mellow
wine	Rosso Conero or Zinfandel

has a nutty and raisin-fruity aroma. The excellent flavor is reminiscent of fruitcake with fudge.

Double Gloucester is made from the whole milk of both evening and morning milking. The key to the original method was that the renneting took place before the milk lost its natural heat. The curds are cut and pressed, and the cheese is matured for four to eight months. Most of the milk is pasteurized today but Christine Appleby in Shropshire and Diana Smart in Gloucestershire use unpasteurized milk. Farmhouse cheeses are made in large flattish cylinders which are cloth wrapped. The paste is a lovely orange color which is not as vivid as some other cheeses which are dyed with annatto. It is much creamier and not as a dry in texture as Single Gloucester. The cheese has a sweet aroma of milky carrots. The flavor is really rich and mellow with raisins and dried fruit, and a lingering lemon acidity.

Serve as a simple snack with salads or fruit or on a plowman's platter with pickled walnuts and red currant jelly. Slices of the cheese were melted into boiling ale and the mixture was thickened with egg yolks and mustard, and poured over hot toast.

Factory-made cheeses are either waxed or wrapped in plastic, and the paste is often colored with annatto. Much of it is mixed with other cheeses and with flavorings such as onions and chives (Abbeydale and Cotswold), bands of Stilton (Huntsman), or sweet pickles (Sherwood).

Smart's Cottage Pie

Mince leftover beef with onion and a little red bell pepper. Bind the mixture with freshly made or leftover gravy and season to taste with herbs, salt, and freshly ground black pepper. Spread out evenly in a heatproof dish. For the topping, boil a pan of potatoes and then mash them with milk and butter, and spoon over the meat mixture. Top with plenty of shredded Double Gloucester cheese and bake in the oven at 400°F until the cheese is melted and the potato is nice and crispy.

RECIPE

Gorgonzola

Northern Italy

There are many tales about the origin of this great cheese from Lombardy but until the early twentieth century it was known simply as "stracchino" or "stracchino verde"—a cheese made from the milk of cattle tired from their long spring and fall treks to and from the Alpine pasture.

As the cheese grew in popularity, a more specific name was needed and the choice fell on Gorgonzola, one of the many villages where such cheeses were made. Today the PDO cheese is made in large factories all over the northeast of Italy.

Gorgonzola is made in drums which vary in size from 13 to 29 lb. It has a thick, coarse reddish-gray crust which may have some powdery patches. The paste is white to pale yellow with a good spread of greenish-blue veins. The texture is quite creamy; more moist than Stilton and more buttery than Roquefort.

milk	Cow's milk
style	Semihard, blue veined, washed rind
fat content	48 %
maturity	3 to 6 months
pungency	Strong
wine	Barolo or Reciota della Valpolicella

The flavor is piquant and spicy, with wood mold and mushrooms, and a bite that gently hits the tongue. The aroma is perhaps stronger than the flavor and an almost alcoholic tang comes from the washed rind. Avoid cheeses which have a sour or bitter smell or which are turning brown.

Serve as an Italian plowman's platter with Italian bread, black olives, and radicchio, or crumble over mixed salad leaves with walnuts. Gorgonzola makes a great cheese course on its own with plain crackers. In Milan, Gorgonzola is used to stuff pears or to make a sauce for pasta flavored with sage and garlic. Try it in soups, potato bakes, vegetable sauces, and stuffings. Mixed with spinach it makes a good stuffing for pancakes.

below: *The piquant flavor of Gorgonzola perfectly complements the earthy taste of mushrooms in a salad.*

Dolcelatte: This is a brand name for a toned-down version of Gorgonzola. The cheese is made at the Galbani factory in Pavia from the curd of one milking, and is sold when the cheese is extremely young. The cheese has a light surface mold and is usually wrapped in foil. The paste is smooth and creamy white with blue-green veins unevenly distributed. The flavor is like a more delicate and mild Gorgonzola.

Gondola: This is a Danish version of Gorgonzola.

Torta San Gaudenzio: This is one of several brand names for Gorgonzola layered with Mascarpone.

American Gorgonzola: Most American-produced Gorgonzola is generally drier and more crumbly than the original, with a sharp, peppery, but not very complex, flavor. An exception is that made by the BelGioioso Cheese Inc. in Denmark, Wisconsin. This is milder than Italian Gorgonzola and more like Dolcelatte.

In days past Gorgonzola was made by adding rennet to the evening milk and then hanging the curds up to dry until the next morning. The following day the curds were put into a mold and layered with curds from the morning milk. This "due paste" cheese is difficult to find today as it takes a year or more to mature and is only made by a few small producers. It has a strong piquant taste much appreciated by connoisseurs.

Factory-made Gorgonzola is known as "una pasta", which is a mixture of the two milks in one layer of curd. The mold growth is encouraged by piercing the curd with copper or stainless steel needles and maturing for half the time of the traditional cheese. The rind is then washed with brine during the ripening process. Young cheeses are sold as "dolce" and more mature ones as "naturale." The result, although sweeter and perhaps more approachable than "due pasta," is still very good. Most reputable manufacturers belong to the Gorgonzola Producers' Association. Their cheeses are easy to recognise as they are wrapped in foil bearing the initials CG which is the Association's mark.

Gouda

This ancient cheese from Zuid-Holland and Utrecht is now largely factory made but you can still find some farmhouse versions. Gouda comes in a variety of sizes, both waxed and unwaxed, and varies in age from a month to two years or more.

Produced in traditional flat wheels, the cheese has a thin yellow rind and a coating of paraffin wax. The young cheese has a firm, pale yellow paste, scattered with small irregular holes or a few larger holes. Factory-produced cheese is soft and springy with a buttery, almost processed, cheese aroma. The flavor is lightly fudgy with nuts but very, very mild.

As the cheese matures, the rind thickens and the paste darkens and hardens, particularly at the edges. The flavor matures to give a much more robust taste. Mature farmhouse cheese has a salty smell with a lovely fruity tang to it and a sweet finish. Cheeses which are aged for more than two years take on an almost butterscotch flavor.

Serve mature Gouda with bread and pickles or include in a cheese buffet. Younger cheeses can be sliced and used in toasted sandwiches, on burgers, or in baked potatoes. Shred the older harder cheeses and use in, Dutch cheese soup, or gratin toppings.

Factory-produced Gouda is made with pasteurized milk and is often dipped in wax to enhance its shelf life. This wax coating varies in color and sometime indicates the presence of flavorings in the cheese such as herbs (green wax) or cumin seeds (orange wax). Some aged Goudas have a black wax coating.

Boerenkase: This is the name for a farmhouse Gouda which is produced in much larger discs than factory-made cheese. It has a golden rind which is not wrapped in plastic or dipped in wax.

Kernhem: This rich and nutty cheese is said to have been invented when a batch of *roomkaas* or cream-added Gouda cheese went wrong. It has a much softer texture than Gouda.

Coolea: The hills of Coolea give their name to this Gouda-style cheese from County Cork in southwest Ireland. Made from unpasteurized milk and matured for six to eight weeks or more, some cheeses are flavored with nettles, herbs, or garlic. The mature cheese is piquant with a lingering flavor.

Penbryn: This is an organic Gouda made in Wales.

Teifi: Patrice Savage-Ontswedder, who trained in The Netherlands, makes a Gouda-type cheese at Glynhynod Organic farm in Dyfed, Wales. The cheese has a floral aroma and a rich flavor. There are twelve different varieties of this cheese including garlic, cumin seed, nettles, and even seaweed.

American Gouda: This is mostly coated in red wax like Edam and it is equally bland and uninteresting. Exceptions are versions made at Bulk Farm, Oakdale, California and Smith's Country cheese, Winchendon, Massachusetts.

Wieninger's Goat Cheese: This young Gouda-style cheese is made from raw goat's milk by Sally and Ted Wieninger near Hunter in the northern Catskill mountains of New York State. The texture is very much harder than cow's-milk Gouda and the flavor is unique.

milk	Cow's milk
style	Semihard, cooked and pressed, natural rind
fat content	48 %
maturity	1 month to 2 years
pungency	Mild to medium
wine	Full-bodied Syrah or Shiraz

Grana Padano

Northern Italy

$\mathcal{G}$rana is the generic name for all Italian finely grained, extra-hard cheeses. They are made from partly skimmed milk and originated in the Po Valley. Grana Padano is made throughout the region, indeed twenty-seven provinces have the right to make it, but it is less well known than its more famous cousin, Parmesan.

The large 53 to 88 lb cheese has a thin, shiny old-gold rind. The paste has a granular texture and it can be sliced when young. As the cheese ages, the paste hardens and breaks up on cutting. It has a deep yellow color which darkens with age. The flavor is excellent, mellow, and intense, strengthening as it matures.

Grana cheeses are traditionally shredded and used as a condiment. In Italy there is hardly a first course that does not have cheese sprinkled or shaved over it. Grana cheeses are ideal for cooking because they melt so well. Use as you would use Parmesan.

milk	Cow's milk
style	Extra hard, cooked, and pressed
fat content	32 %
maturity	6 months
pungency	Medium to strong
wine	Vino Nobile di Montepulciano

Gruyère

Switzerland

$\mathscr{T}$here is no doubt that Gruyère originated in Switzerland, but its use is so widespread in France that the French might be forgiven for thinking it is their own. Indeed, a great deal of this cheese is even produced in France now, but genuine Gruyère can easily be identified as it has the word "Switzerland" stamped all over the rind.

Swiss Gruyère is made from unpasteurized milk in the farming regions surrounding the town of Gruyère in the Canton of Fribourg. It is quite a large cheese with a slightly oily rind which looks a little like wrinkled almond skin or a small honeycomb.

The paste is firm, but slightly softer than Emmental and it feels smoother in the mouth. There are a few small holes scattered through the delicate yellow paste. In older cheeses the paste firms up and turns a slightly grayish yellow. The cheese smells

milk	Unpasteurized cow's milk
style	Semihard, cooked and pressed, natural brushed rind
fat content	45 %
maturity	6 to 10 months
pungency	Medium
wine	Claret

farmyardlike with honey and nuts. The flavor is similar to Emmental with strong peaty tones and a zingy aftertaste.

Although Gruyère is not often served on its own or even with the cheese course, except in Switzerland, it really does have a lot to offer on its own. Serve with crackers and figs or grapes, or in sandwiches with tomatoes and onions. Melted over toast, it makes an excellent accompaniment to fish soup, served to one side or even in the soup. Team up with smoked ham, sliced tomatoes, or if you want to try something different, sliced bananas. Gruyère is, of course, a lovely cheese for cooking. It melts into a beautifully creamy mass in mornay sauces, chicken and veal cordon bleu, and gougères. When used as a topping, it gives an even, not too dry, crust and can also be used with bread crumbs to coat deep-fried vegetables and goujons of fish. It is the traditional cheese used in

below: *Classic Neufchâtel Fondue.*

Fribourg: This is a harder, sharper, and older type of Gruyère that has been aged for two years or more.

Roth Kase: This American cheesemaker based in Monroe, Wisconsin, makes a Gruyère-type cheese with milk which has been very slowly and carefully heat-treated so the flavor is retained.

Heidi Farm Cheese: Frank Marchand is the cheesemaker specializing in Swiss-style cheeses from this Tasmanian producer.

Classic Neufchâtel Fondue

Start by rubbing the fondue dish with garlic. Shred 14 oz each of Swiss Gruyère and Emmental cheese into the dish and mix in 4 tsp cornstarch. Add 1½ cups white wine, a teaspoon lemon juice, and a small glass of Kirsch. Heat the mixture through, stirring constantly so that it does not stick to the bottom of the pan. When the cheese has melted, season to taste with freshly ground black pepper and nutmeg. Serve immediately with a plate of cubes of crusty day-old bread. Alternatively you can dip sliced vegetables into the fondue, such as carrots or zucchini.

RECIPE

the Swiss *sale*, a wonderfully creamy cheese tart that is made in a deep pastry shell.

The best cheeses have a slight dampness in the eyes and fine slits just beneath the rim. This cheese will store well if wrapped up well. To keep it at its freshest, store the cheese in a cool place, wrapped in cloth dampened with salt water, or double wrap in foil and store in the refrigerator.

Gruyère is made in much the same way as Emmental but the curds are less finely cut and are scalded at a higher temperature. Gruyère is then pressed harder and for longer, and ripened at a higher temperature. Unlike Emmental, Gruyère is kept damp with salt water while it matures. This reacts on the rind to accelerate the maturing process.

Gubbeen

Southern Ireland

$\mathscr{T}$his is another cheese where the cheesemaker has opted to switch to pasteurized milk, but the result is still pretty good. Giana Fergusson first made Gubbeen in 1980 from the milk of her husband's herd at Schull in County Cork.

Produced in flat rounds it has a yellow ocher washed rind which develops a strong aroma and taste. The maturing cheeses are washed with salt and water every day for three weeks before sale.

Mrs. Fergusson says that ideally the cheese should be eaten at five to six weeks when the paste starts to run. At this stage the cheese has a nutty and buttery aroma with a lemon tang. The taste is

milk	Cow's milk
style	Soft, brine-washed rind
fat content	40 %
maturity	3 to 12 weeks
pungency	Mild to medium
wine	Red Burgundy or Pinot Noir

clean and smooth with nuts, lemons, and touch of the farmyard. There is a good acidic aftertaste to it. She recommends mixing it with large knobs of butter to spread on pumpernickel bread. Top with pine nuts and broil until the nuts brown.

Haloumi

Cyprus

*T*his is the cheese which you will find broiled in a Cypriot, Greek, or Middle Eastern *meze*. Instead of melting on heating, Haloumi cheese simply hardens. Originating in Cyprus, it is now copied throughout the eastern Mediterranean and may be made from any type of milk. Check the packaging for information.

Like Feta, this cheese is produced in block form and stored in whey brine. Cow's-milk versions are usually vacuum packed. The cheese has no rind and has a springy, rather than crumbly, texture which hardens as the cheese ages. The flavor is milky, sometimes tasting exactly like condensed milk, and less salty than Feta. In Cyprus the cheese is kneaded with chopped mint and cut into blocks.

Serve sliced with olive oil and herbs or fry without oil, as they do in Cyprus and serve with a salad.

milk	Ewe's, goat's, and cow's milk
style	Firm but fresh, brined
fat content	40 %
maturity	A few days
pungency	Mild and salty
wine	Light Beaujolais style

Havarti

Denmark

𝒯his cheese is named for a farm owned by Hanne Nielsen. She was an intrepid nineteenth-century cheesemaker who traveled widely to increase her knowledge of the job. Her cheese is factory made now and is widely distributed.

The paste is supple and creamy with masses of tiny eyes. The flavor is usually exceedingly mild but it strengthens a little as it matures. Some cheeses are flavored with herbs or caraway seeds.

Serve sliced thin for breakfast or use in sandwiches with cucumber and fresh dill weed, mashed dates, or mango chutney.

VARIATION

Top Paddock: This is a farmhouse Havarti handmade by Fred Leppin at Top Paddock Cheeses in Victoria, Australia.

milk	Cow's milk
style	Semihard, cooked but unpressed
fat content	50 %
maturity	3 to 4 weeks
pungency	Very mild
wine	Light Vin de Pays or Beaujolais

Idiazabal

Northern Spain

*O*riginally produced high in the Pyrenees above Pamplona, this rustic ewe's milk cheese was often smoked in the rafters of the shepherds' huts. Today, it is made all over the Basque country in both factory and farmstead, from unpasteurized milk.

The cheese is produced in small drum shapes in varying sizes. The rind is pale yellow in color and quite hard. The paste is creamy white and fairly compact with a few small holes. Smoked cheeses achieve a wonderful golden-brown color and dark ivory paste.

The flavor of unsmoked cheese is mildly farmyardlike with a light sour tang. Smoked cheeses have a delicately smoky and fudgy aroma and flavor but with the farmyardlike tang coming through quite strongly and remaining in the mouth for some time.

Serve sliced with chorizo sausages or Serano ham and good bread, or eat with crunchy fresh vegetable crudités.

milk	Unpasteurized ewe's milk
style	Hard, cooked and pressed, natural rind
fat content	45 to 53%
maturity	2 to 4 months
pungency	Medium
wine	Unsmoked: Red Rioja or Navarra; smoked: White oaked Rioja (Crianza)

Jack

California, US

*J*ack cheese was created in the 1830s by a Scotsman named David Jacks. He made a cheese which was only ripened for about a week to give a very soft and mild white cheese.

Monterey Jack is still made in much the same way. The paste is white and the flavor is mild but lightly tangy. First-class examples include Bear Flag Monterey Jack from the Vella Company and Sonoma Jack from the Sonoma Cheese Company.

milk	Cow's milk
style	Soft, natural rind
fat content	45 %
maturity	3 weeks to over 10 months
pungency	Mild to strong
wine	Californian Chardonnay

VARIATION

Dry Jack: This is Monterey Jack which is aged for seven to ten months and is very hard. It has a sharp, nutty flavor.

English Montery Jack: This has a red wax coating, a yellow paste and a salty flavor.

Kefalotiri

Greece

*K*efalotiri is a well-flavored ewe's milk cheese which is made throughout Greece and the Greek Islands. Most Kefalotiri cheese sold outside Greece is a toned-down version of the cheese, often made with cow's milk, and should be called Kefalograviera.

Versions of the cheese are also made in Cyprus and throughout the Middle East. The Greek has a close-textured creamy white paste with a scattering of little holes and a definite aroma of milky nuts but very little flavor except salt. The Cypriot cheese is much more interesting with a harder, ivory-colored paste. The aroma is stronger with more fudge and less milk. The taste is quite good, too, with mushroomy flowery flavors.

Serve as part of a Greek *meze* dressed with extra virgin olive oil and fresh herbs.

milk	Ewe's, and cow's milk
style	Hard, pressed, natural rind
fat content	45 %
maturity	3 months plus
pungency	Mild to medium
wine	Claret

Lanark Blue

Scotland

*T*his delicious blue cheese from Lanarkshire offers a genuine alternative to Roquefort. It is made by Humphrey Errington on a farm which has Britain's first rotary milking parlour for sheep but after that everything is done by hand.

The cheese has strong greenish-blue veining and a soft creamy texture. There is an attractive herbaceous quality to the cheese with plenty of salt and a tangy aftertaste. Serve with plain crackers or add to a cheese board. Use in place of Roquefort in cooking.

VARIATION

Dunsyre Blue: This is also made by Humphrey Errington from unpasteurized cow's milk. It is aged for three months and has a strong flavor reminiscent of Gorgonzola.

milk	Unpasteurized ewe's milk
style	Semihard blue
fat content	52 %
maturity	3 months
pungency	Medium to strong
wine	Sauternes

Lancashire

*K*ept alive on only a very few farms, real Lancashire is a very different cheese than the creamery product. It is made from unpasteurized cow's milk and has a salty tang which gathers momentum as the cheese matures. By contrast the factory-produced cheese is so mild it is almost tasteless.

The traditional cheeses are made in large cylindrical shapes with rounded edges and are usually cloth bound. The texture of the young cheese is very soft and creamy, and quite difficult to slice because it is so crumbly. The paste is very white in color and has a milky aroma and flavor with a lemon tang.

More mature farmhouse cheeses have a darker primrose paste with a firm, only slightly crumbly, texture. The aroma is really verdant and grassy with just a touch of leaf mold. The flavor is deliciously sharp and mellow at the same time, with complex grassy, fruity tones.

Young Lancashire cheese can almost be spread onto a slice of bread or a cracker. It makes a good sandwich filling mixed with freshly shredded carrots or with chopped dates and walnuts.

The shredded or crumbled cheese melts well and is ideal for making cheese toast. Indeed Lancastrians boast that theirs was the original toasting cheese. At one time it was known as "the Leigh toaster," named for a small Lancashire town where the cheese was made. It is also very good in cheese soup, cauliflower cheese, and traditional Lancashire pies.

The early Lancashire cheesemakers only had a little milk to spare and so they developed a technique for making a large cheese out of more than one day's milking. The curds were often kept for as long as a week or two to encourage the required degree of acidity.

Today Lancashire farmhouse cheesemakers, like Mrs. Kirkham of Goosnargh, still use unpasteurized milk and mix the drained, milled, and salted curd of two or three consecutive days. The curds are milled again, placed in molds, and pressed for 24 hours. They are then bandaged, waxed, and ripened for a few months, depending on the customer.

Lancashire Cheese and Onion Plate Pie

Roll out 12 oz shortcrust pastry and use half to line a 9 in metal or heatproof plate. Soften 1 lb sliced onions in 1 tsp butter and layer on the prepared pastry plate with 1½ cups shredded Lancashire cheese. Season the mixture with salt and freshly ground black pepper, to taste. Cover over with the remaining pastry, pressing down at the sides to seal the filling in. Fork holes in the top and bake in the oven at 375˚F for 45 minutes.

milk	Cow's milk
style	Hard, pressed, natural bandaged rind
fat content	45 to 48%
maturity	3 to 6 months
pungency	Mild to strong
wine	Pinot Noir or Burgundy

Langres

Northeast France

*S*adly this wonderfully pungent cheese from the Champagne region of France is not available in those countries which ban cheese made from unpasteurized milk. At its best it can match any of the cheeses of France.

It is a relatively small cheese produced in tiny 7 oz drums. It usually comes unwrapped and has a sunken top and slightly bulging sides. The rind is the typically bright orange color of a washed rind cheese and this rind gives it its pungent farmyardlike aroma.

The paste is very creamy with a pretty pale yellow color and a sweet aroma of lemons and a touch of bacon. The flavor is strong but creamy. There is a definite suggestion of old socks but this is balanced by a lovely lemony tang.

Serve as part of a cheese course or, if your guests like well-flavored cheeses, on its own with dessert prunes and plain almonds.

milk	Unpasteurized cow's milk
style	Soft, washed rind
fat content	45 %
maturity	3 months
pungency	Strong
wine	Good red Burgundy or mature Moulin à Vent

Le Brouère

Northeast France

*T*his relative newcomer to the cheese scene is the brain-child of the Ermitage creamery in Alsace which normally specializes in making Munster cheese. Le Brouère is essentially a variation of the French Gruyère made in the nearby Jura. Its name is based on an Alsatian dialect word meaning "heath" and refers to the unspoilt pastures of the Vosges mountains.

Le Brouère is made in not quite spherical rounds or wheels about 4 inches thick. It has a light chocolate-brown rind which is embossed with pictures of fir trees and grouse. Each cheese is also numbered and signed. The bright yellow paste is creamy in the mouth and has a firm texture. The cheese is buttery and sweet tasting with nutty overtones.

Serve with fruit and nuts in their shells at the end of a meal or use for cooking. Le Brouère also shreds and melts well.

milk	Cow's milk
style	Hard, cooked and pressed, natural brushed rind
fat content	45 %
maturity	6 weeks
pungency	Mild to medium
wine	Red Burgundy

Leicester

Central England

$\mathcal{L}$eicester was first made by farmers around the city to use up surplus milk left over from the production of Stilton cheese. They added carrot juice to give the cheese its vibrant orange color and so it became known as Red Leicester. In fact, there is only one kind of Leicester and it is all now colored with annatto dye.

Traditionally made like a flat cartwheel, it has a thin, dry rind. The paste is close textured and quite chewy. It has a lightly sweet aroma with nuts and a mild flavor with just a touch of lemony piquancy. Some factory-made cheese is flavored using herbs, garlic, or nuts.

Serve Leicester on a plowman's platter with watercress and scallions or include in a cheese buffet. It is a good melting cheese and gives color to the sauces and soups in which it is used. In its native county, the cheese is sprinkled over milk-soaked bread spread with mustard and baked in the oven.

milk	Cow's milk
style	Hard, pressed, cloth-wrapped rind
fat content	48 %
maturity	3 to 6 months
pungency	Mild
wine	French Vin de Pays

Leiden

The Netherlands

*I*f you like cumin or caraway seeds, you will love this Dutch cheese because one or other is always mixed into the curd.

The cheese is made in flat wheels of varying sizes and authentic cheeses from the town of Leiden (Leyden) carry the city's symbol of two crossed keys. It has a natural yellow rind which may be waxed (in factories) or be rubbed with annatto to give a deep orange-red color (on farms). The paste is similar to Gouda cheese but scattered with seeds. It smells and tastes strongly of cumin or caraway, intensifying as it matures. Serve with apéritifs, ham and pickles.

VARIATIONS

Friesian Clove: Very similar to mature Leiden but flavored with cloves, this very hard cheese comes from the Friesian Islands.

milk	Skim and whole cow's milk
style	Semihard to hard, cooked and pressed, natural rind
fat content	30 to 40 %
maturity	3 months to 2 years
pungency	Very strong
wine	Beer

Limburg

Germany

Strictly speaking this is a Belgian, not German, cheese. It was originally made in the monasteries near Limburg in Belgium but it was adopted, and indeed largely taken over, by the German cheesemakers of the Allgau more than a hundred years ago.

Limburg has the typically pungent aroma of a washed-rind cheese, but the flavor is actually rather disappointing. It seems that it is the rind that is doing all the work! The cheese is produced in small loaves with a reddish-brown rind and a creamy colored paste.

Serve with pumpernickel bread and raw onions. Avoid cheeses which have a slimy rind or where the paste has shrunk—sometimes indicated by a wrinkled foil wrapper.

milk	Pasteurized cow's milk
style	Semihard, washed rind
fat content	30 %
maturity	3 months
pungency	Mild when young to fairly pungent in maturity
wine	Portuguese Garrafeira red

Leiderkranz: This American cheese was invented in 1892 by a German immigrant to the United States, Emil Frey. It was intended to duplicate a popular cheese called Bismark Schlosskase which was being imported into the United States at the time. In the event it turned out rather like a milder and less pungent form of Limburg. It takes its name "wreath of song" from a choral group popular at the time. Today it is quite hard to find. It is sold in small blocks and has a soft, pale brown washed rind and a golden-yellow paste which is quite rich and velvety. The flavor is good, tangy, but not strong.

Old Heidelberg: This is a very similar cheese to Leiderkranz which is produced in Lena, Illinois.

Brick: Brick was invented around 1877 in Wisconsin by John Jossi, a cheesemaker whose family originally came from Switzerland. He wanted to make a cheese with the same aromatic flavor as Limburg but with a firmer texture. He discovered that if he made his curd with a lower moisture content than usual and then squeezed it between two bricks he could obtain the result he wanted. Appropriately enough the cheese is now made in brick-shaped blocks, sometimes with a natural, reddish rind and sometimes in plastic. The paste is very pale in color and firm but supple in texture with numerous small holes. The flavor is usually fairly pungent with tangy and nutty tones rather like a stronger version of Tilsit but not nearly as strong as Limburg. Brick is a very popular cheese to serve with crackers or in sandwiches.

Livarot

Northeast France

$\mathcal{E}$ven well-wrapped Livarot is apt to remind you that it is there! This small cheese from Normandy's Pays d'Auge is certainly a qualifier for the top ten most pungent French cheeses. It used to be made exclusively on farms, but today much of it is made from pasteurized milk in large creameries.

Livarot is known as "the colonel" because of the five strips of raffia which are wrapped round it to stop bulging. It has a glossy orange-brown washed rind which can become very dark and rustic looking. The golden paste has little holes and is soft and springy.

The aroma from the rind is very strong with farmyardlike bacon and ammonia but the paste is more subtle, though still with meaty overtones. The taste is also full and strong with farmyard flavors and a strong, salty lemon tang which bites the tongue. Serve at the end of a meal with apples and pears.

milk	Partially skimmed cow's milk
style	Soft, washed rind
fat content	40 to 45 %
maturity	3 months
pungency	Very strong
wine	Normandy hard cider or Calvados

Mahon

Spain

*T*his distinctively fruity cheese is named for the major town of the island of Menorca. Local farmers have been making cheese here for centuries but its reputation rests on the skill of the local *recogedores-afinadores* or gatherer-ripeners. These experts collect the young cheeses from the farmers and ripen them in underground cellars for two months to two years.

Produced in irregular squares with rounded corners, the young cheese has a golden rind which darkens as it ages. The ivory paste, too, darkens and hardens and develops a scattering of tiny holes. Mahon has a milky sweet and floral aroma. However, the taste is surprisingly sour and slightly tangy with roasted nuts and fudgy toffee remaining on the palate. Serve on a cheese board or in sandwiches, or follow the lead of the Menorcans who serve it sliced, sprinkled with olive oil, salt, and fresh tarragon.

milk	Cow's milk
style	Semihard to hard, pressed, natural rind
fat content	40 to 45 %
maturity	2 to 24 months
pungency	Medium
wine	Red Rioja

Manchego

Central Spain

$\mathscr{T}$his is Spain's best-known ewe's-milk cheese. It is named for the province where it is made—La Mancha, home of Don Quixote. However, it is not as flamboyant as the old windmill fighter. It remains relatively sweet and mild at any age with a touch of salty nuts. Manchego was originally made to barter at livestock markets and it provided durable food for the shepherds who accompanied their flocks on their long annual migrations in search of good pasture. Today, most cheeses are matured for around two to three months and these are sold as *semi-curado*; older cheeses are known as *curado* and then *viejo*. You can sometimes find Manchego *fresco* which has been matured for a much shorter period.

Manchego is produced in squat drums with a distinctive dark straw-colored rind which retains the elaborate pattern of the cheese press. The top and base of the cheese are imprinted with a floral pattern

milk	Ewe's milk
style	Hard, pressed, natural rind
fat content	45 to 50 %
maturity	2 months to 2 years
pungency	Mild
wine	Fino sherry

above: *A windmill in La Mancha.*

[159]

and the sides with the zigzag impression left by the esparto grass (now plastic) binder.

During the ripening period the surface becomes covered with a greenish-black mold. Some cheeses have this rubbed off before they are sold. The deep ivory paste is firm, compact, and perforated with tiny holes. It has an aromatic smell with a hint of butterscotch. This effect is strengthened on the palate together with some nutty tones.

Serve as a cheese course with quince preserves or fresh figs and honey. Alternatively serve on a plowman's platter with black olives and large Spanish tomatoes or add to a *tapas* selection with chorizo and Serano ham.

VARIATIONS

Malvern Manchego: Nick Whitworth at Malvern Cheesewrights in Worcester makes this English ewe's-milk cheese which has a slightly salty subtle flavor.

Berkswell: This is another English ewe's-milk cheese of the Manchego type. It is made from unpasteurized milk by Stephen Fletcher at Ram Hall in the West Midlands. It has a natural beige rind and a close and creamy texture that is also quite crumbly. It is slightly salty with a firm nutty flavor.

Tapas Croquettes

Whisk together 1 Tbsp olive oil, 2 Tbsp flour, and 1/3 cup milk. Cook for 2 to 3 minutes and allow to cool a little. Add 3/4 cup each minced cooked shrimp and shredded Manchego cheese, and season to taste with salt and freshly ground black pepper. Chill the mixture in the refrigerator and then shape it into walnut-size balls. Coat each ball in egg and then dip into bread crumbs. Finally, deep fry them to create crispy, hot croquettes.

RECIPE

Maroilles

Northwest France

Vieux paunt or "old stinker" is the vivid nickname given to this very pungent French cheese from Flanders. It is an ancient monastery cheese and was invented at the Abbey of Maroilles in the tenth century.

Today, it is still produced locally in a variety of shapes and sizes, but the most common are square. The typically orange-red washed rind is recognizable by its rough ridging. It is wrapped and packed in boxes. Ideally you should open the box before purchase to ensure that the cheese is in good shape.

The paste of good Maroilles is soft, bulging slightly but not too much, and with numerous small holes. The aroma of the rind is strong and meaty. The paste has a similar though lighter aroma. The

milk	Cow's milk
style	Soft, washed rind
fat content	45 to 50 %
maturity	4 months
pungency	Very strong
wine	Nuits St. Georges

flavor is excellent with a salty, meaty quality and a lemony tang. It is not a cheese for the faint-hearted. Serve on its own with ripe grapes or on a cheese board.

above: *A cheese board of washed rind cheese. Examples here include (clockwise from top) Livarot, Maroilles, and Epoisse.*

VARIATIONS

Gris de Lille: Also known as "the stinker," this cheese is almost identical to its neighbor Maroilles.

Rollot: This Maroilles-type cheese from the French market town of Rollot in the Somme is said to have earned its maker a pension for life from King Louis XIV of France. The king liked it so much that he appointed him his own personal cheesemaker. Produced in small rounds or heart shapes—also known as Guerbigny—the cheese has a moist orange rind and supple yellow paste scattered with small holes. The flavor is quite strong and spicy.

Boulette d'Avesnes and Dauphin: Originally made by heating buttermilk to precipitate the solids, this cheese was mainly kept for home use. Today it is factory made from failed Maroilles cheeses which are flavored with herbs and spices and hand molded into irregular cones. Some cheese have a very red washed rind, others are tinted. The flavor of the cheese matches its strong color.

Maytag

First made in 1941, this excellent American blue cheese is the result of the joint efforts of the Iowa State University and the Maytag Dairy Farm in Newton. It now enjoys a worldwide reputation, 80 percent of it being sold by mail order and the rest from the farm shop.

The cheese comes in foil-wrapped wheels of various sizes which have had the rind removed. The paste is very white in color with a thick and curdy-looking crumbly texture. The green veining is very well distributed. The cheese may be slightly damp when it arrives but a short spell in the refrigerator dries the cheese and enables it to be carefully cut with a knife. The texture is creamy and almost spreadable.

milk	Cow's milk
style	Semihard blue
fat content	48 %
maturity	6 months
pungency	Strong
wine	Beer

The cheese smells sharply mushroomy with citrus fruits and tastes equally strong, but not unpleasantly so. The flavor is very smooth with complex nutty tones and finishes with a refreshingly sour lemon acidity.

Serve on its own after dinner or mix with cottage cheese to make stuffings for celery stalks, pitted dates, or cucumber boats.

Use in blue cheese salad dressings, dips, and sauces.

Maytag gets its rather unusual texture from its method of production. After the curds are cut they are scooped out of the vats on to "hoops" of cheesecloth which straddle the vat, allowing the whey to drain off. The curds are sprinkled with salt and mold, and rolled back and forth in the cheesecloth to mix. The hoops are then taken to the draining tables and flipped over every 20 to 30 minutes to drain off the rest of the whey.

Fritz Maytag, fourth generation of the Maytag family and now in charge of the dairies, believes that this flipping process allows small holes to remain inside the wheel in which the mold can develop. Pressing would remove them. The cheeses are now salted and left for three days before the mold is helped on by punching more holes in the curd. The wheels go into the curing cellars for the next six weeks. During that time mold develops both outside and in but the outside mold is removed and the cheeses are waxed prior to storage in another, colder, cellar. This is where the flavor of the cheese really develops. Just before the cheese is ready, samples are taken, and the cheese is then punched again, the wax removed, and then the cheese is packed.

Milleens

Western Ireland

his is one of the most exciting washed-rind cheeses to come out of Ireland in the last few years. It is made by Norman and Veronica Steele on their farm in West Cork. The milk comes from their own cows and those of two neighbors and the cattle graze the lower mountain slopes of Mishkish mountain that overlooks the Atlantic.

The cheeses are made in 3 lb and 8 oz discs. They are matured on the farm for two or three weeks. Some shops sell it straight away, others mature the cheese for another four to six weeks.

Milleens has a wonderfully pinkish-orange washed rind and a firm to creamy paste. The aroma, as you would expect from a washed-rind cheese, is farmyardlike but the flavor is rich with sweet floral tones which linger on the palate.

Serve on its own as a cheese course or with soda bread and Irish stout. Or slice on a salad with asparagus spears and rolls of Parma ham.

milk	Unpasteurized cow's milk
style	Soft, washed rind
fat content	45 %
maturity	4 to 10 weeks
pungency	Medium
wine	Chardonnay

Mimolette

Northwest France

*L*ooking rather like an orange soccer ball with a light powdering of snow, the mature cheese has a strange, rather rubbery texture and distinctive flavor. The rind is fairly smooth in the young cheese but, as it ages, it becomes thick and deeply pitted. Cheese mites proliferate in these pits to give the characteristic powdery appearance of the older cheese.

The paste is dyed to a deep orange color which darkens toward the rind. The texture is firm and breaks rather like fudge. The young cheese has a relatively mild aroma and flavor but aged cheese takes on a strong, distinctive, almost medicinal smell. The taste of the mature cheese is strong and tangy with citrus fruits and baked nuts.

Serve on a mixed cheese board as a piquant alternative to milder cheeses or eat with black bread and sweet-sour cornichons or cucumbers. Mimolette shreds well and can be used in cooking.

milk	Cow's milk
style	Hard, pressed, natural brushed rind
fat content	45 %
maturity	2 months to 2 years
pungency	Medium to strong
wine	Beer

Morbier

*A*t first glance this cheese from the Jura looks as though it has a band of mold running through the middle of it. In fact, it is ash or charcoal. In the past the cheese was made from leftover curd from other cheeses. The first day's curd was preserved by a layer of ash until the next day's curd was added.

In those days Morbier was made on farms on the lower slopes of the Jura during the winter months. Today most Morbier is factory made from one batch of milk, with the ash added for decoration.

The best cheeses are made from unpasteurized milk—labeled *lait cru*. They are made in flattish cylinders with a grayish-brown rind and bulging ivory paste. They have a meadowsweet aroma of nuts and hay. Serve as a snack with crackers or use in sandwiches with a sweet chutney. Morbier shreds quite well and gives a light cheese flavor to baked vegetables and sauces.

milk	Cow's milk
style	Semihard, pressed, natural brushed rind
fat content	45 %
maturity	2 to 3 months
pungency	Mild
wine	Alsace Pinot Gris

Mozzarella

Southern Italy

*R*eal Mozzarella is made from buffalo's milk. There have been herds of buffalo in Campania in the region to the south and west of Naples since the second century AD, except for a brief spell during the war when the retreating Nazis destroyed them.

Buffalo-milk Mozzarella is thriving again but there is also a good deal of Mozzarella being made from cow's milk not only in Italy but in a number of other countries as well. However, there is really no comparison between the two. Buffalo-milk Mozzarella has a much softer and less rubbery texture and a far better flavor. It is well worth the extra time and cost of seeking it out.

Italian Mozzarella is produced in small, almost oval-shaped balls and it is stored in bowls or in sealed bags of whey. Most non-Italian Mozzarella is sold in small rectangular blocks. All Mozzarella is very white in color with a very thin shiny skin. The texture of the young

milk	Buffalo's or cow's milk
style	Soft, cooked and stretched
fat content	45 %
maturity	1 to 3 days
pungency	Very mild
wine	California Chardonnay or Chablis

Bocconcini: These are very small Mozzarella cheeses, usually made from cow's milk. They are displayed on the counter in bowls of whey. Serve tossed in chopped herbs with extra virgin olive oil.

Bufala Provola: This is a yellow smoked cheese from Campania made from Mozzarella which has been smoked with burning straw in a cylindrical container.

Mozzarella Affumicata: This a smoked version of the cheese which is made in much larger balls so that they will not fall apart as they are being smoked. The cheeses are hung up in barrels while wood chippings of various kinds are burnt below them. The cheeses take on a charred brown to black appearance.

Scamorza: This is a denser type of Mozzarella made in Piedmont as well as southern Italy. It is also made in Dallas, Texas, by the Mozzarella Company. Here the cheeses are smoked over burning pecan shells.

above: *Mozzarella and Tomato Salad.*

cheese is quite elastic and supple and can be sliced reasonably easily. As it ripens, it becomes rather softer. It also increases in flavor. However, you should not allow this process to go too far or the cheese will deteriorate.

Buffalo-milk Mozzarella is worth serving on its own, although cow's-milk versions usually need beefing up with other flavors. Serve sliced buffalo-milk Mozzarella with a good extra virgin olive oil or with a few red berries or a kiwi fruit. Use in the classic tricolore salad with sliced tomatoes and avocados, or serve with sliced oranges and olives, or with roasted bell peppers and strips of sundried tomatoes.

On cooking, Mozzarella becomes extremely stringy and it is the first choice of cheese to use in pizzas. It is also a classic ingredient in *Mozzarella in Carozza*. Here the cheese is placed in a sandwich, dipped in egg and milk, and fried.

Mozzarella is a spun-curd or "pasta filata" cheese. A starter and rennet are added to coagulate the milk, and the curds are cut into fairly small pieces and allowed to settle. The curd is then lifted out of the whey and kneaded in hot water until it forms a smooth shiny mass. Small pieces are cut off and shaped into individual cheeses which are then brined and packed ready for sale. When buying Mozzarella cheese, make sure the shopkeeper gives you sufficient whey to keep the cheese damp. If the Mozzarella is in a bag, check that the whey has not seeped away.

Eggplant Pizza

Mix a 14 oz can of tomatoes with 1 Tbsp tomato paste, a crushed garlic clove, a pinch of dried oregano, and salt and pepper. Boil until fairly thick, stirring occasionally. Cut 2 eggplant into about 16 slices. Brush with olive oil and place under a broiler. Broil for 8 to 10 minutes, turning occasionally. Spread the tomato mixture onto the broiled eggplant slices and top with slices of Mozzarella. Return to the broiler and cook for 2 to 3 minutes until the cheese bubbles.

RECIPE

Munster

Northeast France

$\mathcal{T}$he rolling hills of Alsace not only produce excellent spicy wines, they also produce this very pungent cheese. Its production center is the pretty village of Munster set amid pastures and vineyards. Munster must come from this area to qualify for its PDO status.

Munster comes in small rounds, packed in protective, wooden boxes. Some cheeses are now also packed in smaller unboxed sizes but they do not have the full texture and flavor of the large ones.

The young cheese has a thin but firm pinkish-red rind with white paste. As it matures the rind turns to a dark russet color with a deep straw-colored interior. The paste is soft and supple with small holes in it. It becomes almost creamy in texture as it matures.

The rind has a strong farmyard aroma with a lemony tang to it and this flavor transfers itself to the paste which is also strong in

milk	Cow's milk
style	Soft, washed rind
fat content	45 to 50 %
maturity	1 month
pungency	Strong
wine	Alsace Gewürztraminer

flavor and has a robustly meaty taste to it.

Serve at the end of a meal with fruit and Alsacian wine. Add a small bowl of caraway, cumin, or fennel seeds for everyone to sprinkle on the cheese as they eat it. In Alsace this cheese is never far away from one or other of these spices.

Avoid cheeses which have matured too far. These have an even stronger and unpleasant smell of the stables. The rind will be dull, cracked, and slimy, and the paste runny.

VARIATIONS

Gerome: An identical cheese from Lorraine which is just slightly larger in size.

Lingot d'Or: Another variation on the Munster theme, this time from Contrexeville, a town made famous for its mineral water. Lingot d'Or means "gold bar" and that is exactly what the cheese looks like.

Chaumes: Named for the high pastures of the Vosges mountains but factory made in southwest France, this pleasant but relatively mild cheese has only a hint of the complex nutty flavors of Munster. Chaumes has a tough yellow-brown rind and a golden-yellow paste with a few holes and firm rather elastic texture. The flavor of this cheese is full and creamy with gentle nutty tones.

German Münster: There are a number of villages in Germany which go by the name of Münster but none of them are home to this factory-made cheese. German Münster is firmer in texture and larger than the French cheese. It has a pleasantly strong flavor but without the complexity of the original.

American Muenster: This is a very bland cheese, its only virtue being that it melts extremely well.

Ossau-Iraty-Brebis Pyrénées

Southwest France

*A*lso known simply as Iraty, this is a Basque cheese, but from the French rather than the Spanish side of the Pyrenees. It was originally made from unpasteurized goat's milk but is now widely copied in French creameries.

It is produced in medium-size cylinders with rounded sides. The rind is a smooth grayish beige. The paste is pale yellow in color with a supple texture. It has small holes and fissures scattered through it.

It has a distinctive, sour, winelike aroma with a touch of the farmyard and a really tangy, spicy taste. Lemons and leaf mold remain in the lingering flavor which is sweet, salty, and mellow.

Serve as part of a cheese board with apples, pears, or grapes. Use in salads and sandwiches, or serve with sliced Bayonne ham and *saucisson sec*. Iraty is not used much in cooking in its native region but it is very good shredded into baked potatoes or into risotto.

milk	Ewe's milk
style	Hard, pressed, natural brushed rind
fat content	45 to 50 %
maturity	3 months
pungency	Medium
wine	Cahors

Parmigiano-Reggiano

Northern Italy

$\mathscr{I}$n the English-speaking world this famous cheese is generally known as Parmesan. It is the classic cheese used in the great cuisines of France, and the rest of the world has followed suit. Parmesan is a member of the Grana family of very hard Italian cheeses and it has been produced in small-size dairy farms or *caselli* in the Po Valley for many hundreds of years.

Today more than two million cheeses are produced every year, but they can only be made under strict regulation in certain designated regions of the province of Emilia Romagno. They are made in squat drums which look rather like small beer barrels. The rind is a shiny golden brown color and has the name of the cheese printed all over it. The paste is a good straw-yellow color with a grainy, flaky, and brittle texture which hardens as the cheese matures.

The cheese has a radial grain which makes it difficult to cut with a knife. Instead it is split open with a special wide-bladed tool and irregular pieces are broken off. The aroma of Parmesan is unmistakable. It is full of sharply defined raisins and dried fruit with wine. In a good cheese the flavor is wonderfully full and fruity with a salty tang. There are crunchy casein crystals and a lingering aftertaste.

Most people think of Parmesan as a condiment to sprinkle over pasta, soups, and other dishes, or to use in cooking, but it also makes a very good dessert cheese, particularly when it is young or middle-aged. The Italians serve it in chunks with figs or pears, or break it into even smaller pieces to eat as an appetizer with their apéritifs.

In the kitchen it is extremely versatile. Thin shavings add interest to salads and are classic with thinly sliced Bressaola, Carpaccio, or raw artichoke hearts. Shredded, it is used on all pasta sauces except those made with fish. It goes into pesto sauce, soups, and vegetable dishes such as eggplant with Parmesan. As well as having an excellent flavor, Parmesan also melts perfectly without any hint of stringiness. It can be used in almost any dish which calls for cheese and is often mixed with other cheeses to add flavor. Try it with Cheddar in cauliflower cheese, with Gruyère in cheese soufflé, or with Asiago in macaroni cheese.

Because of its long maturation, Parmesan is much more easily digestible than many other cheeses. In Italy, very young children, old people, and sportsmen and women are all encouraged to use Parmesan regularly.

above: *Parmesan shredded into Coriander and Pasta Soup.*

Many people buy ready-shredded Parmesan in packages or cardboard tubs. This is a mistake because the cheese in these packages bears no relation to that cut from the whole cheese. Parmesan loses its flavor fast when it is shredded, and so it should always be bought in blocks and shredded at home as and when required. Ideally you should only buy where you can see the piece cut from the whole cheese, but this is not possible for everyone.

Genuine Parmesan cheeses are not only stamped with the name of the cheese but also with the year the cheese was made. Export cheeses also carry an export mark so that the cheese can be traced back to the producer. Parmesan is sold at one of four stages:

Giovane – young, after fourteen months

Vecchio – old, after eighteen months to two years

Stravecchio – mature, after two to three years

Stravecchione – extra mature, after three to four years

You may prefer the cheese at any one of these stages or you may want to use cheeses at different levels of maturity for different culinary purposes. However, Parmesan is said to be at its peak when it is *congocciola*; this means that when the cheese is split open you can just see tiny tears of moisture glistening on the surface. In the right conditions Parmesan will keep for a long time. At home you can wrap it in a piece of damp cheesecloth, and then in foil, and store it in the refrigerator for up to two months.

Parmesan cheese is made only from unpasteurized milk between April 1 and November 11, but so much is made, and the cheeses are matured for so long, that there is always plenty on sale. It takes 35 pints of milk to make $2^{1}/_{4}$ lb of cheese.

Production starts by mixing the previous evening's milk with the partially skimmed morning milk. A starter culture is added and the milk is heated. When the lactic acid reaches the required level, rennet is added. Coagulation occurs quickly and the curd is turned and broken up with a special sharp-edged tool, known as a *spino* or thornbrush, into pieces the size of wheat grains ready for cooking.

After the curds are heated, they fall to the bottom of the cheese kettle to form a solid mass. The curds are removed in cheesecloth, placed in molds, and lightly pressed. The cheeses are then stamped with the name, brined, and stored for ripening.

After fourteen months the cheeses are tested and graded. The testers work with a percussion hammer, a screw needle, and a sampling dowel but their technique is such that they rarely need the latter. They start by knocking the cheese with the hammer and then listen carefully to the reverberations. This tells them what is going on inside the cheese, and from this they decide which of five quality levels the cheese has reached. The diagnosis is confirmed by the use of the screw needle, which gives an indication of the degree of resistance in the cheese, and a small sample to smell and taste. Once graded the cheeses will either be sold or will go on to mature for a longer period.

milk	Unpasteurized whole and skim cow's milk
style	Extra hard, cooked and pressed, naturál brushed and oiled rind
fat content	28 to 32 %
maturity	1 to 4 years
pungency	Medium to strong
wine	Chianti Classico Riserva

Pecorino

*I*n the the hills of central and southern Italy, cows are rare. Instead ewe's milk is used to make hard compact cheeses which are generally known as Pecorino. Each region has its own type.

Pecorino may be sold fresh, medium, or mature, and the rind tends to vary in color depending on the whim of the producer. Some, like Pecorino Senese, are brushed with tomato paste and others, such as Pecorino Romano, are rubbed with oil and wood ash.

Fresco or young cheeses usually have a very white paste which can be quite crumbly in texture. The paste darkens and hardens as the cheese matures. Really mature Pecorino can be very hard with casein crystals.

Aromas and flavors, too, change as the cheese matures. The young cheese can be quite mild with just a light touch of lemon, whereas older cheeses can be extremely piquant and salty. Almost all cheeses have a touch of nuttiness and the characteristic lemony tang of a ewe's-milk cheese.

Serve young cheese on a cheese board or on an Italian plowman's platter with olive bread, radicchio, and plum tomatoes. It is also very good sliced and served with strips of sundried tomatoes and olive oil. In the early summer Tuscans eat their Pecorino with fresh fava beans from the pod.

More mature Pecorino cheese is made for shredding and is used in the regional dishes of southern Italy. Try it in stuffings for tomatoes, mushrooms, and other vegetables.

Pecorino Toscano: This version from Tuscany is very often eaten while it is still young, when it is almost creamy in texture. Older cheeses harden and take on a more chalky texture. Some Pecorino Toscano are made from mixed milks, so look for the words *tutti di latte di pecora* or *latte pecora completo* which signify that only ewe's milk has been used.

Pecorino Romano: This version from Lazio must be matured for at least eight months before it is sold, though it is usually eaten when it is even more mature. It has a particularly salty and piquant flavor which comes from six to eight weeks of dry-salting. Shred or shave off slivers and serve with salami and bread, nibble with olives, or sprinkle over pasta. Always buy pieces cut from the whole cheese. Never buy Pecorino Romano preshredded.

Pecorino Sardo: When it is mature this Sardinian cheese is very similar to Pecorino Romano although expert cheese-tasters can tell the difference. However, a good deal of the Pecorino Romano on sale is really Pecorino Sardo! The young cheese is also eaten after two or three weeks.

Pecorino Senese: This is really a Tuscan Pecorino but its rind is often rubbed with tomato paste instead of the more usual oil and wood ash.

Pecorino Siciliano: This Pecorino from Sicily is also known as Canestrato or Incanestrato. This name refers to the basket pattern which the molds give to the rind. Pecorino Siciliano has a very sharp flavor which is sometimes strengthened even more by mixing saffron or peppercorns into the paste. Very young Pecorino Siciliano is also eaten the day after it is made when still unsalted. Known as Tuma, it has a very delicate taste and a soft, creamy texture.

UK EWE'S-MILK CHEESES

There are a number of small producers of ewe's-milk cheese which have sprung up in the last ten years or more on farms and in small dairies around the UK. The cheeses tend to be more akin to young rather than mature Pecorino. Distribution is mostly limited to specialty cheesemongers and farm shops.

Duddleswell: This truckle cheese made from unpasteurized ewe's milk at Sussex High Weald Dairy at Uckfield. It has a light creamy taste. Some are flavored with chives or crushed peppercorns.

Redesdale: Sold either when it is relatively young and delicate or at four months when it is strong and fully flavored, this ewe's-milk cheese is made· by the Northumberland Cheese Company at Otterburn. Some cheeses are flavored with herbs.

Ribblesdale: This small red-waxed cheese has a nutty flavor. Some are smoked over oak and ash to make Ribblesdale Smoked cheese.

Spenwood: This prize-winning cheese, made by Village Maid in Berkshire, has a very distinctive full flavor which has been compared to young Parmesan. It is made from unpasteurized ewe's milk. It is matured for six months and has a natural rind and hard texture.

Tala: This new cheese is named for Tala Water, a small stream which runs through a hidden valley near Launceston in Cornwall. The cheese is made from the farm's own milk by Heather White. It has a natural rind and firm primrose yellow paste. It has a buttery aroma with wine and nuts and a similar sweet-sour taste with roasted nuts and good tangy length. There is also a smoked version which has a harder texture and smoky bacon flavor.

Tyning: Surprisingly similar in style to Italian Pecorino, this prize-winning cheese is made by Mary Holbrook at Timsbury, near Bath. Made from unpasteurized ewe's milk, the cheese is matured for six to twelve months.

American Pecorino: Lucie and Roger Steinkamp make a semisoft and mild Pecorino-style cheese and a year-old version at La Paysanne Inc. in Hayward, Minnesota. They also produce a smoked version. Another serious contender is Idaho Goatster from Karen and Chuck Evans at Rollingstone Chevre in Idaho.

Picodon

Southern France

$\mathcal{E}$verywhere you go in the south of France you will find a version of these attractive little goat's-milk cheeses. They are usually made in small 3 to 4 oz drums and are sold at various stages from young and creamy to old and extremely hard. The best are the PDO cheeses of l'Ardeche, on the eastern side of the Rhône valley, and those of la Drome, on the opposite side. Avoid cow's-milk copies which are made by some large creameries in the area.

Picodon has thin natural rind and a good white paste. As it matures the rind and the paste harden. The flavor, too, intensifies to a medium-sharp nuttiness. Some young cheeses are pierced and soaked in the local *eau de vie*; or packed in olive oil with herbs.

Serve Picodon on its own with crusty bread and fruit. Roast whole cheeses in the oven and serve on bed of salad leaves. Sprinkle with raisins soaked in balsamic vinegar and toasted pine nuts.

milk	Goat's milk
style	Semihard to hard, natural rind
fat content	45 %
maturity	1 to 6 weeks
pungency	Medium
wine	Côtes de Provence

Pont l'Évêque

Northwest France

$\mathcal{T}$his pungent cheese is still made on the farms of the Pays d'Auge in Normandy just as it has been for centuries. You will find the farmhouse or *fermier* version on country market stalls and in the local shops. However there are also some large creameries using pasteurized milk to make quite a reasonable *laitier* version of the cheese.

Pont l'Évêque is made in a distinctive square shape which is achieved by cutting the curds into blocks rather than into small pieces or grains. One block makes one cheese. They are drained and placed in square molds. After dry-salting, the cheeses are ripened in humid cellars.

milk	Cow's milk
style	Soft, washed rind
fat content	45 to 50 %
maturity	6 to 8 weeks
pungency	Pungent
wine	Rioja Reserva or Calvados

The maturing cheeses are washed with brine to give a light tan-colored rind which develops the characteristic pungency of the cheese. Indeed the aroma is strong enough to qualify the cheese for the top ten most pungent French cheeses, but it should not be so strong that it is unpleasant.

The yellow paste is supple with a few small holes. The aroma from the rind is strong but not overpowering. There are farmyard smells with bacon and ammonia. The paste has a much milder aroma reminiscent of nuts. The flavor is relatively mild and sweet, with grassy herbaceous tones and shortbread cookies.

Serve as a cheese course with grapes and water biscuits. In cooking its flavor goes very well with potatoes; it is very good on baked potatoes or layered with onions and potatoes and mushrooms in a casserole.

above: *Potato and Mushroom Bake.*

VARIATIONS

Pavé d'Auge or Pavé de Moyeaux: These are larger, stronger versions of Pont l'Évêque which are ripened for longer—maybe three to four months. The paste is firm and full of small elliptical holes. The flavor can be rather bitter.

Calvador: This is a brand name for a milder, rather watered-down version of Pont l'Évêque made in a small disc shape.

Vieux Pane: This is a creamery invention which is loosely based on Pont l'Évêque. It is square and has an orange washed rind with crisscross markings from the mold. It has a pale yellow, fairly springy paste and if kept for too long will start to run slightly. The flavor is fairly full but not as complex as Pont l'Évêque.

Port Salut

Northeast France

*P*ort Salut started off life at the other side of France at the Breton abbey of Port-du-Salut at Entrammes. It was a popular cheese and so, in 1938, the monks registered Port Salut as its trade name to protect it from imitations. Then, after the Second World War, the monks decided to sell the name to a large factory producer. So Port Salut is now made in Lorraine and the monks sell their own cheese under the name of Entrammes.

Produced in medium-size flat discs, Port Salut has a tawny washed rind and a smooth, springy yellow paste. Both the aroma and flavor are very mild with just a hint of earthy nuttiness to them. It is a very easy-eating cheese which can be used in all kinds of everyday catering.

Serve in chunks with fruit or raw vegetable crudités. Slice and use in sandwiches with sweet pickles or serve melted in a steak sandwich (see right).

right: *Ciabatta Sandwich with Steak.*

VARIATIONS

Saint-Paulin: This cheese was one of the original imitations of the monks' Port-du-Salut. Today it is made by another French factory creamery and is virtually identical to Port Salut.

Père Joseph: This is a Belgian factory-made semihard cheese inspired by Port Salut. It has a distinctive black wax coating and pale yellow paste with a scattering of small holes. The flavor is quite pleasantly full with a nutty aroma.

Oka: This was once a monastery cheese made by the monks who emigrated from Brittany to Canada at the end of the nineteenth century. They carried on making their Port Salut-style cheese at a monastery at the village of Oka near Montreal. Today it is made by Canada's largest dairy cooperative but it is still matured in the cellars of the monastery. The cheese has a better, less rubbery texture than its French cousin and a more interesting flavor.

Ridder: This relatively new cheese from Scandinavia is very much in the Saint-Paulin/Port Salut mold. It is produced in flat wheels with an orange, washed rind and deep yellow paste. The texture is very buttery and the flavor slightly nutty.

Trappist: This is a general term for a monastery-style cheese originated by Trappist monks and includes Port Salut and Saint-Paulin. According to some authorities Trappist is also the name of a cheese first produced in Bosnia in 1885.

milk	Cow's milk
style	Semisoft, washed rind
fat content	45 %
maturity	1 month
pungency	Mild
wine	Bergerac or Valpolicella

Provolone

Southern Italy

*T*his is the most popular cheese in southern Italy and no kitchen is likely to be without it. It is a "pasta filata" cheese like Mozzarella but, instead of being eaten while it is young, it is brined and hung up to dry. The result creates a very different cheese indeed.

The plastic curd lends itself to improvisation, so Provolone comes in all shapes and sizes from cottage loaves to torpedo shapes. Some cheeses are sold as young as two months, but six months or more is a more usual maturation period.

Young Provolone is mild and lightly spicy. Older cheeses have a deeper straw-colored paste which can develop small cracks. A really good Provolone has a strongly herbaceous aroma with salad leaves and a lemony tang. The taste is rich and spicy with the same attractive herbaceous flavors and a salty bite.

Serve young Provolone in slices on a plate with other cheeses, or with olives and spicy radishes as an appetizer. Use in sandwiches with sliced tomatoes and raw onions. Older cheeses shred well and can be used in all kinds of cooking. Try it in cheese gnocchi.

milk	Cow's milk
style	Hard, "pasta filata," natural rind
fat content	45 %
maturity	2 months to 2 years
pungency	Medium to strong
wine	Chianti Classico

VARIATIONS

Burrini, Butirro, and Burri: These are all local names for small pieces of Provolone which have been shaped into an oval with a small chignon on top. They may be smoked or shaped round nuggets of sweet butter. They may be eaten young or aged.

Burrata: These are larger than Burrini but similar in that pieces of Provolone paste are wrapped in a bag shape round a mixture of Mozzarella and cream and the bag tied with raffia or twisted closed. They are eaten very young.

Caciocavella: A short pear-shaped cheese from Campania in southern Italy made to a similar recipe to Provolone.

Provolone Piccante: This is Provolone which has been matured for a year or more. These cheeses take on a hot peppery flavor.

American Provolone: Most American Provolone is beige in color, pliant, and mild, and is really more like factory-made Mozzarella than real Provolone. The exception is that made by the BelGioioso Cheese Inc. in Denmark, Wisconsin. Errico Auricchio is the fourth generation of his family to make cheese but he is the first one to do so in North America. He and his family moved to the United States in 1979 and set up the company which specializes in making Italian-style cheeses from authentic Italian recipes and the Provolone is excellent. They sell a "sharp" Provolone which is aged for seven months and an "extra sharp" which is aged for a year or more.

Pastorello: This is an Australian stretched curd cheese made on Donnybrook Farm in Victoria. It is a hard cheese with a good sharp flavor to it.

Pyrénées

Southwest France

$\mathcal{T}$he most important cheeses of the Pyrenees are the indigenous ewe's-milk cheeses, but an important cow's-milk cheese industry has sprung up on the lowlands. A number of creameries make large quantities of semisoft cheeses which they have invented themselves. All these types of cheeses have very bland flavors and a great many of them are sold for export.

Usually labeled "Fromage de Pyrénées," these cheeses are produced in rounds or discs with a firm but supple yellow paste with lots of small holes scattered through it. The rind may be painted or waxed in various colors. The flavor of all of them is very mild indeed.

milk	Cow's milk
style	Semihard
fat content	50 %
maturity	1 month plus
pungency	Very mild
wine	Chablis or light Chardonnay

Well-distributed brand names include Doux de Montagne (brown waxed), Saint Albray (pale orange rind), Lou Palou, and Le Capitoul. Serve sliced with other cheeses or cut into batons for salad. Use to flavor fish pies and mornay dishes.

Raclette

Switzerland

*T*he name Raclette means "scraper" and refers to a group of cheeses which are melted to make a traditional Swiss dish of the same name. These are mountain cheeses made originally in the Vallais but now all over Switzerland.

Raclette cheeses are produced in wheels about half the size of Gruyère with beige to brown rinds and dark ivory to yellow pastes. The texture of most Raclette cheeses is very smooth and it seems to melt in the mouth even without heating. The aroma is strongly reminiscent of the stableyard with fruit and wine. The taste is usually equally strong, with rich winelike notes, and a tangy accent.

In Switzerland Raclette cheeses are not usually served uncooked but they are very good sliced and served with airdried ham. When cooked the cheese melts to the lovely velvety mass which is used so effectively in Raclette.

milk	Unpasteurized cow's milk
style	Semihard
fat content	45 %
maturity	2 to 3 months
pungency	Strong
wine	Beaujolais

Reblochon

Northeast France

*F*or many years the existence of this cheese was a well-kept secret within the Haute-Savoie. It was made from milk which was withheld (*lait de rebloche*) when the tax collectors came to check the milk yields. The farmers did not milk the cows dry. They then finished the milking after the inspectors had gone. This milk was made into a cheese for home use.

milk	Cow's milk
style	Soft, washed rind
fat content	50 %
maturity	7 to 8 weeks
pungency	Medium
wine	Claret

Today Reblochon is also produced in commercial dairies from pasteurized milk. The cheeses are made in small pinkish-gray discs with a washed rind. The paste is very supple with a number of small holes. It has a fairly pungent aroma but a mild, fruity, and creamy flavor which is quite excellent. Serve as a cheese course on its own with celery or radishes and fine claret. Deep fry in bread crumbs and serve with homemade fruit chutney.

Ricotta

Italy

*R*icotta is a byproduct of Italy's huge cheesemaking industry. It is made from the whey that is left after the curds have separated out. For many years whey posed something of a problem as it was not easy to dispose of. Then it was discovered that if whey was heated, the casein particles in the whey would fuse together to create a new curd. Drain this curd and you have Ricotta.

Ricotta is sold as a fresh white cheese with a granular consistency. In local shops in Italy it is often shaped like an upturned basin with basketwork marks on the outside, but most of it is sold in plastic tubs. The flavor is mild and sweet.

Serve at the cheese course sprinkled with salt and pepper and chopped fresh herbs or berry fruits. Use in open sandwiches with shrimp, or in salads with melon and prosciutto. Ricotta is also used widely in Italian cooking in pasta dishes.

milk	Cow's, ewe's, goat's milk, and whey
style	Fresh
fat content	Very low
maturity	Fresh
pungency	Mild
wine	Sparkling wines or Champagne

Robiola

Northern Italy

*R*obiola is the general name given to creamy fresh cheeses made in the sparkling wine producing region of Asti in Piemonte. One of the best known comes from the hillside town of Roccaverano. The milk from local cows, ewes, or goats may be used according to availability.

The cheeses are made in rough rounds and wrapped in paper. Small versions are known as Robiolina. There is no rind and the soft, moist paste is startlingly white. The aroma is sweetly milky with a touch of lemons which strengthens on the taste to an attractively sour finish. The cheese is quite salty. Occasionally the cheeses are brushed with mustard and matured for three weeks. These cheeses have a sharper and more definite flavor.

milk	Cow's milk
style	Soft, fresh
fat content	50 %
maturity	Fresh
pungency	Mild to medium
wine	Prosecco

Robiola spreads easily onto bread or crispbreads and can also be served with salads including fresh fruit. Use in cooking to give a creamy consistency to soups, sauces, and pasta dishes.

Roquefort

Central France

$\mathcal{T}$his great French blue cheese has a history going back to before the Dark Ages. It was known to the Romans in the first century AD and has been praised by emperors, kings, and poets. In 1411 a royal charter of Charles VI gave the people of Roquefort the monopoly of curing the cheese in the local caves at Combalou, and this charter has been upheld ever since.

Roquefort is made from unpasteurized ewe's milk and its popularity is such that the local flocks can no longer produce enough milk to fulfil demand. Corsica has come to the rescue and hundreds of cheeses are shipped to the mainland to be ripened in the all-important Combalou caves.

Produced in 5½ lb drums, the cheese has virtually no rind. It is closely wrapped in foil. The paste is very white in color with a uniform bluish-green veining throughout. The texture is firm, smooth, and almost spreadable. The aroma is milky with nuts and fruity raisins. The flavor is

right: *Salad with Roquefort Dressing.*

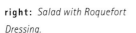

salty with delicate complexity and a tangy finish. Cheeses made for the French market are often less salty than those for export.

Serve on its own with celery or grapes or add to a cheese board or buffet. Make a plowman's platter with baguette and dessert pears or with whole-wheat rolls and watercress. Roquefort is an excellent cheese to use in any recipe which calls for blue cheese. Its subtle flavor will not overwhelm the other ingredients. Use to make blue cheese salad dressings, tartlet fillings, stuffed canapés, and sauces for steak and veal.

When buying Roquefort, avoid cheeses with a crumbling edge or which do not have a great deal of blue-green veining. The best cheeses are classified as "Surchoix." Roquefort keeps quite well in the fridge. Wrap in foil and store in the salad compartment.

Roquefort is not a complicated cheese to make but great care is taken to ensure that it maintains its quality. The process starts with the mixing of the morning and previous evening's milk. This mixture is curdled with rennet. After two hours the curds are cut and ladeled into draining molds with perforated sides. The Penicillium mold is added at this stage.

After a week in a special room where they are turned frequently, the cheeses are carefully removed from their molds and sent to the caves at Combalou. Here they are brined and pierced to allow the moist air in the caves to get into the cheeses and encourage the mold growth. The cheeses remain in the caves for at least three months and maybe more depending on when they are required in the market.

The caves were formed when the Combalou mountain collapsed and they were built in their current state in the seventeenth century. The circulation of air in the caves is regulated naturally through the *fleurines* or cracks in the rocks which occurred when the mountain collapsed. The caves therefore have a stable temperature and humidity.

milk	Unpasteurized ewe's milk
style	Semihard blue
fat content	45 %
maturity	3 to 6 months
pungency	Strong
wine	Châteauneuf-du-Pape or Sauternes

Noodles with Roquefort and Walnuts

Cook some fresh noodles, drain very well, and keep warm. Mix equal quantities of Roquefort and light cream in a pan and place over medium heat. Allow the mixture to melt, making sure it does not stick to the bottom of the pan and bring to just below boiling point. Pour over the prepared noodles and toss well with some chopped walnuts and freshly ground black pepper.

RECIPE

Sainte-Maure

Central France

*T*his attractive little log-shaped goat cheese is made in both Poitou and Touraine. The latter cheeses are characterized by the presence of a length of straw or stick running through the length of the cheese.

The cheese has a white downy rind which hardens and starts to blue as it matures. The paste is firm but spreadable with a full slightly "goaty" flavor which strengthens as it ages. It is entirely a matter of personal preference at which stage you decide to eat the cheese.

Serve as part of a cheese board or on its own with crusty bread and tomatoes. Use in soups and sauces for an unusual but interesting flavor. Surprisingly, the "goatiness" of the flavor tends to fade when the cheese is heated.

milk	Goat's milk
style	Soft to hard, natural rind
fat content	45 to 50 %
maturity	2 to 8 weeks
pungency	Medium
wine	Chinon

VARIATIONS

Sainte-Maure Cendre: This is a version of the cheese which has been rolled in ash.

Ragstone: This is an English goat cheese log which is similar to Sainte-Maure.

Saint-Nectaire

Central France

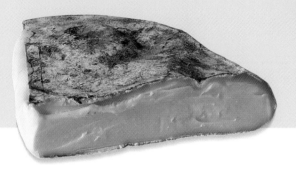

*D*espite its AOC (now PDO) status, this ancient French cheese from the mountains of the Auvergne is now mainly factory produced from pasteurized milk. This has resulted in a real loss of flavor, the factory conditions are so sterile that the bacteria which normally grow on the rind and add to the flavor are inhibited.

The cheese is made in large round flat discs. It has a grayish rind with light yellow or reddish patches. The supple paste is pale gold in color and becomes almost runny as it matures. It has a really earthy aroma. The paste alone has a sweet and grassy aroma and this is repeated in the flavor which is only slightly farmyardlike. Factory-made Saint-Nectaire remains firm, though supple, with a moldy smell and a mild flavor.

Serve as part of a cheese board or slice and serve in open sandwiches with French airdried sausages or salami.

milk	Cow's milk
style	Semihard, pressed, natural rind
fat content	45 %
maturity	2 months
pungency	Mild to medium
wine	Côtes du Rhône

Samsoe

Denmark

$\mathcal{S}$amsoe started off life as a Danish version of Swiss Emmental but today it has developed a totally different character of its own. Once a farmhouse cheese, Samsoe and its many descendants are now factory produced.

Made traditionally in round flat cartwheels, and now also in large slabs, Samsoe has a golden-yellow dry rind which is usually coated in yellow cheese wax. Softer than Emmental, it has a texture which can be flabby but which at its best is more akin to Cheddar.

The paste is pale yellow in color with a few shiny holes about the size of cherries. The flavor is quite mild and nutty in the young cheese, but this strengthens and takes on a slightly more pungent quality as the cheese matures. However, it still does not reach the complexity of flavor achieved by Emmental. Samsoe is a useful cheese for those who do not like strong flavors because it is very

milk	Cow's milk
style	Semihard, cooked and pressed, natural rind
fat content	45 %
maturity	3 to 6 months
pungency	Mild to medium
wine	Light Vin de Pays red

versatile. It offers a mild alternative on a cheese board and, sliced with a handheld cheese slicer, it mixes well with other sliced cheeses. Use slices, also, to make open sandwiches, typical of the Danes, with fruit and light pickles. Cut into slivers for salads and mix with shredded ham, cornichons, and celery root for an excellent chef's salad. The Samsoe family of cheeses melt well, giving a slightly stringy result which is good in toasted sandwiches or melted over asparagus toasts or on poached eggs.

above: *Mix Samsoe with Danish Blue to make a Danish Cheese Mousse.*

V A R I A T I O N S

Danbo: This is a particularly bland member of the Samsoe family. It is sometimes spiced with caraway seeds which gives it a good deal more flavor.

Elbo: This is a rectangular version of Samsoe which has a red wax coating.

Fynbo: This is a smaller and milder cheese than Samsoe with fewer and smaller eyes in the paste. Its main claim to fame is that it comes from the island of Fynbo which was the home of Hans Christian Andersen.

Sovind: This new cheese is made to a traditional Danbo recipe in much the same way as Cave cheese (see page 89) but without the bacterial culture. The cheese is matured in a store utilizing the salty winds of the North Sea. It is a little firmer than most of the Danish yellow cheeses. It has numerous small holes in the paste. The flavor is rather like a mild Cheddar.

Tybo: This cheese is very like Elbo but with smaller holes in the past.

Sapsago or Schabzieger

Eastern Switzerland

*T*his pale green cheese from the Canton of Glarus is something of an acquired taste. It is made from skim milk and buttermilk and flavored with fenugreek and melilot, a wild clover which grows in the locality and gives the cheese its unique flavor.

Sapsago has many names and may even simply be referred to as "green cheese." It is pressed into small truncated cones weighing about 3½ oz called "stockli." The cheese is extremely hard and is made for shredding. The flavor is reminiscent of salad leaves, sage, and mixed herbs. Use Sapsago to flavor salad dressings, dips, or pasta dishes.

milk	Skim milk and buttermilk
style	Fermented, pressed, no rind
fat content	3 %
maturity	Fresh
pungency	Very strong
wine	Beer

Sbrinz

Switzerland

*L*ittle known outside Switzerland, this extra-hard mountain cheese takes almost twice as long to mature as Emmental or Gruyère. It is more like an Italian Grana cheese and will keep for a long time without requiring a cool environment.

Produced in large flattish wheels, Sbrinz has a hard, thick, golden-brown rind and an extremely hard, grainy paste. The aroma is very tangy and piquant. The cheese has a very distinctive aroma with rich coffee and chocolate tones and a lemony tang. The flavor is really mellow and mature with a slightly burnt quality to it.

Sbrinz is very good shaved into paper-thin curly slices and served with apéritifs or on a bed of bitter salad leaves. Shredded, it melts well into cooked dishes, giving an attractively piquant taste. It is used in a traditional mountain dish of noodles and diced potatoes, baked with onions and cream, and topped with Sbrinz.

milk	Unpasteurized cow's milk
style	Extra hard, pressed, natural brushed rind
fat content	45 %
maturity	2 to 3 years
pungency	Mellow to medium
wine	Alsace Pinot Blanc

Selles-sur-Cher

Central France

$\mathcal{T}$he Loire valley is home to this little goat's-milk cheese from the village of Selles-sur-Cher near Orléans. It is one of the many local village goat cheeses in the area but is distinguished by the fact that it is always coated in black ash.

Produced in tiny 3½ oz discs, the cheese has a very white paste in contrast to its black surround. The paste is firm yet soft and moist when it is young. The flavor is mild and nutty. As the cheese matures it develops a soft blue mold under the ash and the paste hardens and sharpens in flavor.

Serve as part of a cheese course or spread onto bread, crackers, or crispbreads. Serve on its own with fruit or salad. Use the young cheese to stuff ripe figs and serve as an appetizer with a vinaigrette flavored with rosemary.

milk	Goat's milk
style	Soft to firm, natural ashed rind
fat content	45 %
maturity	3 to 4 weeks
pungency	Mild
wine	Sancerre

Shropshire Blue

England

*D*espite its name this relatively new cheese has nothing to do with Shropshire. It was invented and produced in Scotland but is now made by some of the Stilton cheese producers. Indeed, it is made in exactly the same way as Stilton except that annatto is added to the milk with the starter culture and the mold.

The cheese comes in medium-size drums with a rough brown rind. The paste is bright orange in color with vivid blue veining. The texture is firm and creamy, but also slightly crumbly. The flavor is sharper than Stilton and quite distinctive. There is a definite sour or winelike tang with oranges and lemons but the aftertaste is sweet.

This cheese looks really dramatic on a cheese board or buffet but it is also very good served on its own. Use sparingly to give a color lift to stuffed baked potatoes and chicken Cordon Bleu.

milk	Cow's milk
style	Semihard blue, natural brushed rind
fat content	48 to 55 %
maturity	3 months
pungency	Medium
wine	Claret

Stilton

*S*adly there is no farmhouse Stilton today and even the smallest producer—Colston Bassett—changed to pasteurized milk some time ago. Much of the art of the traditional Stilton cheesemaker has been taken over by technology and the clock. However, Stilton still has a first-class flavor, though perhaps somewhat mellower and more approachable than it used to be.

Stilton is named for the little village of Stilton, but it has never been made there. It was, however made nearby and is still made locally within the counties of Derbyshire, Leicestershire (now including Rutland), and Nottinghamshire. Known in Britain as the "king of cheeses," Stilton has been protected by a copyright invested in the Stilton Cheesemakers' Association. There are currently five members of the association and one other producer.

Stilton cheeses are drum shaped with a thick, hard, uncracked

milk	Cow's milk
style	Semihard blue, natural brushed rind
fat content	48 to 55 %
maturity	3 to 18 months
pungency	Strong
wine	Port

crust which is usually grayish-brown and slightly wrinkled with whiteish powdery patches. The paste is crumbly when young, softening and darkening at the rind as it matures. It is a lovely creamy ivory color with well-spread blue veining growing from the center outward. The veining increases in area and turns a bright blue-green with maturity.

The aroma is sharply nutty and the flavor is full of mellow nuts and fruit. The flavor strengthens as it matures.

Stilton is not sold until it is at least three months old and a few cheeses are sold when they are more mature. The best Stilton, made from the summer milk, is in the shops from September to Christmas. The age at which Stilton should be eaten is very much a matter of personal preference, but much of the cheese sold in supermarkets is fairly immature. More mature cheeses are to be found in specialty cheese shops.

Stilton is a good after-dinner cheese. It was traditionally served with Port. At one time it was fashionable to slice the top off a whole cheese and to spoon or scoop out the paste with a special scoop. Sometimes the cheese was also pierced with knitting needles and Port was poured over the cut surface and encouraged to penetrate into the cheese.

Scooping Stilton from the top is now frowned upon by the experts who suggest that the cheese should have large wheels cut off the top which are then cut into wedges to serve. This method stops the cheese drying out round the sides as the hole in the center deepens, but it is much less fun!

Stilton is now equally popular as a snack or as part of a plowman's platter with bread

above: *Stilton crumbled onto a salad.*

and pickles and maybe a glass of beer. It makes a good open sandwich or canapé topping, an excellent addition to salads, and a filling for baked potatoes. Stilton is quite difficult to shred but it will melt straight into soups and sauces. Potted Stilton, made by mixing with softened butter, brandy, and a dash of nutmeg, makes a very good butter for broiled steaks or cutlets.

Buy Stilton from a whole cheese. If you buy a large piece, cut it into useful sizes and double wrap with plastic wrap and foil to freeze. Thaw for 24 hours, not in the refrigerator, before serving. The smaller truckles do not have the same flavor as the larger cheeses.

Stuffed Mushrooms

Gently fry 4 or 5 fine chopped shallots in plenty of butter. Process 5 oz white bread to make crumbs and add the shallots and butter together with 4 oz Stilton, some chopped fresh sage and parsley, and seasoning. Mix well and use to stuff 11 oz open cap mushrooms which have  *had their stems removed. Place on a baking sheet and bake at 325˚F for 35 minutes.*

RECIPE

White Stilton: It is occasionally possible to find some white Stilton. This will always be a very young cheese as Stilton will always have a tendency to blue naturally. Good versions have an attractive lemony sour tang to them. Bad ones have little flavor at all.

Flavored Stilton: There is a range of Stilton cheeses which are layered with other cheeses, such as Cheddar or Double Gloucester, and other flavorings. These are simply a way of using up Stilton cheeses which might not make the grade on their own.

Jumbunna: This is an Australian Stilton-style blue cheese made by Fred Leppin at Top Paddock Cheeses in Bena, Victoria.

All Stilton is made from pasteurized milk. A starter culture is used and this is followed by the rennet. Once the curd is set, a couple of hours later, it is cut both vertically and horizontally into long ribbons which look rather like square tagliatelle or into cubes and then left to settle again. The Penicillium mold may be added to the milk or to the curds.

The next stage is a move to large drainers where the curd is left to stand for 24 hours, before being cut again into blocks and then broken down by hand into pieces the size of tennis balls. Once the curd is drained, it is milled and salt is mixed in by hand. It is very important to get an even distribution of salt. The salted curd is spooned into hoops and turned regularly until it is time to move the cheeses to the cheese store. Here they are pierced two or three times to encourage the blue veins to grow until the cheeses are graded at about twelve weeks.

Taleggio

Northern Italy

*T*aleggio is one of the oldest of soft cheeses. It was being made by families in and around the small town of Taleggio near Bergamo in Lombardy as long ago as the eleventh century.

The cheeses were made in the fall and winter when the cows came down from the Alpine pastures into the villages. The milk was taken from the cows when they were tired—stracche in the Lombardy dialect—after the long journey and the cheeses came to be known as Stracchino cheeses.

Today both factory and farmhouse versions of Taleggio can be found. Most cheeses are made in 8-inch squares, but some cheeses may be larger. The cheese has a deep pinkish-orange washed rind which is fairly thin when young but which thickens with darker striations as it ages. It should not be cracked.

The paste is pale ivory and supple, with a few holes here and

milk	Cow's milk
style	Semisoft, washed rind
fat content	48 %
maturity	6 to 10 weeks
pungency	Medium
wine	Chianti Classico Riserva or Recioto di Soave

there. The best farmhouse versions have an exotic aroma of raisins, nuts, and tangy lemons, with farmyardlike tones. The cheese melts in the mouth as you eat it and the taste is beautifully full and fruity, with roasted nuts going into a long and creamy finish.

Serve Taleggio on its own as the star of the cheese course with walnut bread and the fruit bowl. Or serve as a snack with bitter salad leaves and very ripe tomatoes. Taleggio melts well and it is excellent sliced over polenta or mixed into risotto. Use on bruschetta for a different flavor with roasted zucchini and sage.

Factory-produced Taleggio is increasingly being made using a modern cooked-curd method which creates cheeses more like Italico cheese (see page 64). The paste of these cheeses is much whiter in color and the flavor is very mild in comparison to a good farmhouse Taleggio.

above: *Chicken and Zucchini Risotto with Taleggio.*

VARIATION

Robiola Lombardia: These are a group of small Taleggio-like cheeses which are sold under a variety of brand names.

Formaggio Fritto

Cut the cheese into ¼-inch thick slices and lightly dust with flour on both sides. Coat with beaten egg and then dip into bread crumbs. Fry in butter or oil and remove with a slotted spoon. Serve immediately with a fresh green salad. In Lombardy Taleggio cooked in this manner is often served with fried eggs and bread.

RECIPE

Tête de Moine

Switzerland

*T*ête de Moine means "monk's head." The cheese was originally invented by the monks of Belleray Abbey in the Bernese Jura, and the brothers taught the local farmers how to make it. It is only made from the rich summer milk and tradition has it that the first cheeses are ready to eat when the first leaves of fall drop from the trees.

The cheese is now made by cooperative dairies in the region and is sometimes known as Belleray cheese. Unlike most other mountain cheeses which tend to be very large, it is made in small drums about the size of a 28 oz can of vegetables.

The rind may be smooth and slightly greasy, or rough and brown in color. The paste is firm and creamy to straw-yellow in color, darkening as it ages. There may be small holes or horizontal fissures in the paste. Older cheeses smell strongly of roasted nuts with

milk	Cow's milk
style	Semihard, pressed, natural brushed rind
fat content	50 %
maturity	4 to 6 months
pungency	Strong
wine	Northern Rhône reds

above: *As with all Swiss cheeses, the label on the top clearly marks the name and country of origin.*

winelike stable aromas. The flavor is sweet and tangy, with musty wood mold and nuts.

Traditionally the cheese is served in thin sliced curls with black pepper and ground cumin, so look for cheese crackers flavored in this way. Serve Tête de Moine with a platter of airdried meats, with vegetable crudités, or with fruit.

Tête de Moine can be sliced vertically but to get the frilly curls of cheese which are served in Switzerland you will need to use a *girolle*. The curls are achieved by turning the handle of this special knife on a stand and shaving the cheese across the top and a little way down the sides. This gives the cheese a look which resembles a tonsure which may have contributed to its present name.

Tetilla

*L*ooking just like a child's spinning top, this wide conical cheese from Galicia is made from the milk of cows grazed on the lush pastures behind the coastal mountain range. The local cheesemakers used to shape it by hand but most Tetilla is now made in large creameries and it gets its shape from plastic molds. However, this transfer to mass production does not always spoil its flavor.

The cheese has a thin yellow rind with a slightly greenish cast. The pale yellow paste has some irregular holes. It is an elastic paste and easy to slice. The cheese smells of milky meadows. It has an attractively creamy melt in the mouth. The flavor is full of fudge and nuts with a lemon sour tang to it.

Serve Tetilla thin sliced with Serano ham and chorizo sausages and a glass of Fino sherry. Use it to make interesting open sandwiches with broiled vegetables or sliced artichoke hearts in oil.

milk	Cow's milk
style	Semisoft, pressed, natural rind
fat content	45 %
maturity	8 to 10 weeks
pungency	Mild to medium
wine	Sherry or Cava

Tilsit

Germany

*T*ilsit was the invention of Dutch immigrants to the town of Tilsit in East Prussia, first Soviet Sovetsk and now Lithuania. Since then it has been widely copied and is made all over Germany. In the east of the country it is also known as Tollenser.

The traditional shape for Tilsit is a large wheel but, increasingly, the cheese is being produced in large loaf shapes which are convenient for slicing machines. The cheese has a thin brownish rind and creamy yellow paste with numerous apertures scattered through it.

The texture is very springy and elastic but fairly moist. Some cheeses, particularly those made in the loaf shape, have a mild and lightly tangy flavor, but the better cheeses have a big and attractively spicy taste.

Tilsit is a versatile cheese and the Germans traditionally serve it thin sliced for breakfast, cut into chunks in salads and for snack lunches, as well as in a large wedge on a cheese board after dinner. It toasts well and makes an excellent topping for hamburgers. Tilsit is also good for cooking and can be melted into cheese sauces for pasta, flans, and potato dishes.

milk	Low-fat cow's milk
style	Semihard, cooked curd, natural washed rind
fat content	30 to 50 %
maturity	6 months
pungency	Medium
wine	German beer

VARIATIONS

Swiss Tilsit: This cheese used to be exported under the name Roy-alp. It is perhaps rather more like Appenzell than German Tilsit for it has fewer larger holes and is firmer. The taste, too, is different with a more earthy, farmyardlike edge to it.

Tilsit Havarti: This is a milder-flavored version of German Tilsit which is made in Denmark.

Kardella: This is an Australian version of Tilsit made at Top Paddock Cheeses in Victoria, Australia.

Bremen Toast

Toast slices of well-flavored rye or whole-wheat bread and steam some asparagus spears until tender. Melt a little butter in a frying pan and fry pork or veal medallions on both sides for 4 to 5 minutes. Place 2 medallions and some asparagus spears on each piece of toast and top with sliced Tilsit cheese. Place under the broiler and cook until the cheese begins to bubble.

RECIPE

Tomme de Savoie

$\mathcal{T}$his is one of the best of the many French "Tomme" cheeses. It is made in Savoie and the Haute-Savoie near to the Swiss border. "Tomme" means "piece" and is a general word for semihard cheeses made by specialty cheesemakers.

It has a rustic appearance and a distinctive hard, powdery rind varying in color from grayish-white to pinkish-brown. The paste is pale ivory in color, darkening at the rind, and supple with a few small holes scattered through it. The aroma is strongly grassy with ammonia, mushrooms, and caramel. The flavor is much sweeter with a fudge taste and a citrus tang.

Beware of Tomme de Savoie lookalikes which have a smooth rind and a very boring taste. Look for the words "fabriqué en Savoie" rather than "affiné en Savoie" on the authentic cheeses.

Serve with bread and salad or fruit. It is also good for toasting.

milk	Cow's milk
style	Semihard, pressed, natural rind
fat content	20 to 40 %
maturity	2 months
pungency	Mild to medium
wine	Beaujolais

Vacherin Fribourgeois

Switzerland

$\mathcal{N}$ot to be confused with Swiss Vacherin Mont d'Or, this cheese from the Valais is a semihard cheese with a wonderfully full and nutty flavor, rather like Italian Fontina.

Vacherin Fribourgeois is made in large wheels about 12 to 16 inches in diameter. It has a distinctive brown rind which is coarse textured and greasy. The paste is pale yellow with small holes scattered through it. The cheese has a strong farmyardlike and cookie-like aroma. The flavor, too, is reminiscent of the farmyard with sweet hay and bacon tastes ending in a rich caramel finish.

Young cheese called Vacherin à Main is served mainly as a dessert cheese. Older cheese, made from winter milk, is called Vacherin à Fondue and is used with Gruyère in *moitié-moitié* or half-and-half fondue. It melts at a lower temperature than usual so can be used for nonalcoholic fondue with water in place of spirits.

milk	Unpasteurized cow's milk
style	Semihard, pressed, natural washed rind
fat content	45 %
maturity	3 to 6 months
pungency	Medium
wine	Rioja

Vacherin Mont d'Or

Northeast France

$\mathcal{V}$acherin Mont d'Or is named for a mountain in the Jura which straddles the Swiss/French border. However, in 1973 the Swiss commandeered the name for their version of the cheese and so the French PDO cheese is sold as Vacherin du Haut Doubs and other versions as Le Mont d'Or.

This cheese in unusual as it uses unpasteurized winter milk to form the soft wonderfully aromatic and velvety cheese. Most cheeses need meadowsweet summer milk to reach this level of flavor. Sadly it is illegal to export Vacherin Mont d'Or made with unpasteurized milk to the United States.

Vacherin Mont d'Or is made in very flat cylinders varying in size from 5 to 12 inches in diameter. Each cheese is girdled in spruce or fir tree bark and sold in boxes made of thin pinewood. This practice not only holds the cheese in shape—it can be very runny when it is mature—it also gives the cheese a distinctive resiny flavor.

milk	Cow's milk
style	Soft, mold rind
fat content	50 %
maturity	3 weeks to 2 months
pungency	Medium
wine	Riesling

The cheese has a white mold which ripens to a pale pinkish-brown and which ripples like waves across the top surface of the cheese. The paste is very pale with a slight greenish cast when it is young and it has a number of small holes through it. It is soft and

spreadable when young but to get the best effect and flavor you should eat it when it is fully ripe and runny. It has a fairly mild and milky aroma, which is very pleasant but is nothing compared to the stunning flavor of sweet grassy meadows with a touch of farmyardlike leaf mold.

The traditional way to eat a ripe Vacherin Mont d'Or is to cut off the top rind and to eat the runny cheese out of the center. In the Jura, people make a complete meal of it with boiled potatoes and cumin seeds. Sometimes wine is poured over the top and the box is wrapped in foil and baked in a hot oven for 20 minutes.

Serve a whole cheese at the cheese course with simple crackers and a good fruit bowl. Alternatively spread a little of the cheese on squares of toast and melt in the oven. Serve with Riesling.

VARIATION

Swiss Vacherin Mont d'Or: This is almost identical to French Vacherin Mont d'Or, made on the other side of the Jura mountains in Switzerland, but it is made from pasteurized not unpasteurized milk. It is therefore legal to export it to the United States. The dairies which make this type of Vacherin are situated in the valley of Joux so the cheese may also be called Mont d'Or de Joux.

Valençay

Central France

*T*he story goes that Valençay was first made for the French statesman, Talleyrand, who owned the Château de Valençay in the Cher valley. Also known as Pyramide, it is made in a truncated pyramid. It can be found in the summer and fall months on sale at almost every farmhouse in the area. Creamery-made cheeses are younger and are on sale all year round.

Valençay has a natural beige rind which is blacked with ash. The paste is smooth and white and fairly moist when it is young, hardening to a shredding consistency when aged. The aroma is not very goatlike but earthy with a citrus tang. The flavor is very mild but with a sharp lemony tang on the finish. Older cheeses strengthen in flavor.

Serve on bread or with toast for lunch or supper, or add to a cheese board or buffet.

milk	Goat's milk
style	Soft to firm, natural rind sometimes ashed
fat content	45 %
maturity	4 to 5 weeks
pungency	Mild to strong
wine	Californian Fumé Blanc

Wensleydale

N o r t h e a s t   E n g l a n d

*W*ensleydale cheese has had a checkered history in recent years but the tradition of making it actually in Wensleydale continues at a small creamery in Hawes in northwest Yorkshire and on a few farms. The cheese was first made by the monks at nearby Jervaulx Abbey with milk from their herds of sheep and goats.

Wensleydale cheeses are drum shaped and may be cloth bound or waxed, depending on their size. The cheese has a natural thin and dry pale yellow rind. The paste is a pretty pale primrose color and is firm but crumbly. The aroma is fragrantly sweet and milky with a lovely grassy note. The taste is very similar with a citrus tang which sharpens to tart apples and an attractive lemony aftertaste.

Fruitcake, gingerbread, and apple pie are the traditional accompaniments to Wensleydale cheese. Indeed a local rhyme illustrates the point.

milk	Cow's milk and small quantity ewe's milk
style	Hard, pressed, natural cloth-wrapped rind
fat content	45 %
maturity	2 to 6 months
pungency	Medium
wine	Chardonnay

"Apple pie without cheese
Is like a kiss without a squeeze."

However, the cheese goes equally well with bread and crackers on a plowman's platter or after dinner. Serve with fresh fruit, like pears and grapes, and eat as soon after purchase as possible. Wensleydale also cooks very well. Use to make cheese biscuits, cheese soup with celery, stuffed mushrooms, and crumble toppings.

Made from pasteurized milk from farms within a ten-mile radius of the creamery, Wensleydale cheese is made with a vegetarian rennet. The curds are cut, scalded, and cut again into large blocks. They are then salted and shredded through the cheese mill, before being packed into molds, and very lightly pressed. The cheeses are then bandaged and stored in the drying rooms before being matured for two to six months.

VARIATIONS

Smoked Wensleydale: Wensleydale cheeses are matured and then smoked for 24 hours to give a delicately smoky flavor to the cheese.
Blue Wensleydale: There was a time when most Wensleydale was blue veined and this is a return to that tradition. The flavor is quite mild and creamy. This cheese is very good melted with scallions on toast or in baked potatoes. This cheese is sometimes smoked.

Panaggerty

This Northumberland specialty is very good made with shredded Wensleydale. Heat some cooking oil in a 7-inch deep frying pan. Layer 1 lb potatoes, sliced very thin, with 8 oz sliced onions and 4 oz Wensleydale cheese in the pan, starting with the potatoes. Cover with a lid and cook over low to medium heat for a half hour until the base is very well browned and the potatoes are tender. Finish off under a hot broiler.

RECIPE

index

credits and acknowledgments

Picture credits

p. 7, p. 13 e.t. archive; p. 9 H. J. Errington & Co; p. 10, p. 31, p. 194 Food & Wine from France Ltd; p. 12, p. 25 Easter Weens Farm, Bonchester Bridge; p. 14 Westbury Communications Ltd; p. 15 Osbourne Publicity Services Ltd; p. 16, p. 17 Italian Trade Centre; p. 18, p. 211 Cheeses from Switzerland Ltd; p. 19 Dutch Dairy Bureau; p. 21, p. 46, p. 79, p. 159 Foods from Spain, Spanish Embassy Commercial Office; p. 22, p. 161 Maytag Dairy Farms, Iowa; p. 26 Jacqui Hurst; p. 32, p. 28 (left) Colston Bassett & District Dairy Ltd, (right) Alvis Brothers Ltd, Lye Cross Farm; p. 29 J & L Grubb Ltd; p. 30, p. 43 The Highpoint Partnership; p. 205 Westbury Blake; p. 211 Gregory, Ellis, Martin & Partners Ltd.

Acknowledgments

The Publisher would like to thank the following for their contributions to the making of this book: La Fromagerie, 30 Highbury Park, London, for providing many of the specialist farmhouse cheeses used in the directory; Divertimenti, London, for providing the tools and equipment used for photography; and for supplying additional information about the various cheeses— Tillamook County Creamery, The Austrian Trade Commission, Ticklemore Cheese, Easter Weens Farm, Field MacNally Leathes PR on behalf of Boursin, Louis and Jane Grubb at Lye Cross Farm, J.L. & E. Montgomery, S.H. & G.H. Keen, Mrs. Appleby of Broad Hay Farm, Lynher Valley Dairy, High Point PR on behalf of MD Foods plc, Mrs. Smart of Smarts Gloucester Cheese, Gubbeen Farmhouse Products Ltd, H. J. Errington & Co, Wensleydale Dairy Products Ltd, Besnier Ltd.